Praise for the Kite Meth

Thanks to Guila's Kite Method, we saw measurable results in the form of quicker class design, better retention from our learners, and significantly lower stress levels for our designers. The Kite "ties it all together" for both trainers and developers.

Scott Wuerch, *Former Training and Quality Manager*
GSI Commerce

Guila's dynamic approach to teaching instructional design reaches all learning styles. Through it, my colleagues and I have discovered new insights and effectiveness to training design and delivery. I refer again and again to the Kite Method. Guila is a muse!

Katharine Heumann, *Office of the Commissioner*
Alaska Department of Environmental Conservation

Thanks to the Kite Method, our participants continue to improve performance long after the session is over. It's a winner!

Babette Lisotta, *Director of Training*
Zones, Inc.

Because our SMEs developed the curriculum themselves, we spent less than one-quarter what we would have if we had used a consultant. Our development time was cut by a third!

Barbara Courtney, *Former Director*
Artist Trust

Guila inspired us to enjoy the opportunity we have to teach and share with our customers and colleagues. It was an invigorating experience that positively impacted our entire process.

Drew Sheminski
Carl Zeiss IMT

Guila transformed our docents into professionals that presented with confidence! Thanks to Guila's passion and expertise, the entire docent program is an unequivocal success.

Dan Smith, *Resource Manager*
George P. Johnson Experience Marketing

Guila time and time again ignites our attendees with her innovative approach to designing courses for adult learners in the public sector.

Leslie Fritz, *CPRP, Director of Education*
California Park & Recreation Society

Guila's groundbreaking approach to designing classes for adult learners has resulted in improved classes for both the trainer and the participants. We see a marked difference—participants are now engaged, eager to learn, and carry the concepts well past the class.

Theron Powell, *Program Coordinator, Quality Assurance Unit*
Alaska Juvenile Justice

INSTRUCTIONAL
DESIGN

that
Soars

Shaping What You Know
Into Classes That Inspire

GUILA MUIR

BOOK PUBLISHERS NETWORK

Book Publishers Network
P.O. Box 2256
Bothell • WA • 98041
Ph • 425-483-3040
www.bookpublishersnetwork.com <http://www.bookpublishersnetwork.com>

10 9 8 7 6 5 4 3 2 1

Printed in the United States of America

LCCN 2013900104
ISBN 978-1-937454-73-9

Interior and cover designed by Sara Schneider

Contents

PART ONE

Instructional Design
That Soars

You will find truth more quickly through delight than gravity.
Let out a little more string on your kite.
Alan Cohen

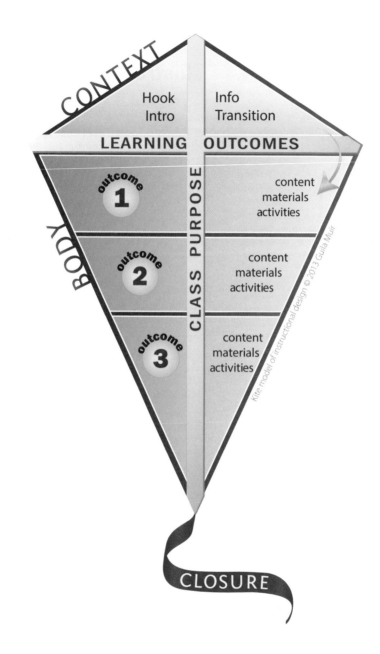

Chapter 1

Why a Kite?

- Has your boss asked you to develop training in a specialized topic?
- Do you have a passion to teach and don't know where to start?
- Do you need to train many people in a short period of time?
- Are you tempted to just download the content in your brain into a slide show?

There is a better way!

Transform your expertise into inspiring, engaging training sessions with the Kite Method. Used by thousands of people to impact organizations and communities, the Kite Method gives you all the skills you need to launch your class, seminar, or corporate training session and to keep it aloft.

When I first studied instructional design (ID), I found it laborious. I wondered, "Where is the *fun*?" Traditional models of the instructional design process often looked something like this.

Traditional Instructional Design Process: Example

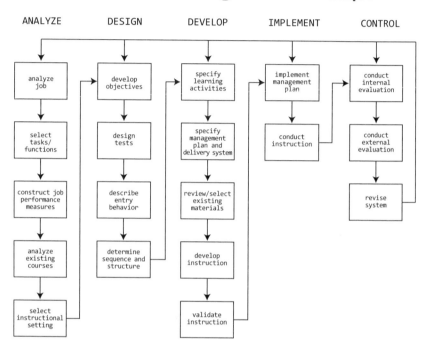

Although simplified models were developed, many people still needed streamlined, step-by-step guidance to keep up with the constantly shifting needs of their workplaces and communities.[1]

While teaching people to develop training, I discovered that the kite metaphor took a direct route to my students' brains. It enabled them to easily grasp even the most complex concepts of instructional design.[2] My students found it surprisingly fun to develop lively training sessions that got results.

My goals are to make the instructional design process as easy and fun as possible. You, too, can develop classes that teach your students effectively—and have a great time building and flying your unique Kite.

What I've Learned in Twenty-five Years

I am the founder of Muir and Associates, one of the premiere train-the-trainer firms on the West Coast of the United States. In that role, I have helped thousands of people with an astounding diversity of knowledge transform into great trainers. I've always been fascinated with how to develop training sessions that are not only energetic and fun but also change the way people think and act.

As I voraciously read, learned, and taught, I continued to challenge myself to simplify the instructional design process while retaining its "must-dos." The result is the Kite Method.

You Won't Just Build A Kite—You Will Fly It!

You don't need to get a certificate in instructional design to create great classes. The Kite Method makes it easy. It distills the essential elements of instructional design and adult learning to enable you to design and teach both onsite classes and Webinars. The Kite template is so easy to use that once you build your first Kite, you can easily build others on any topic in the world.

Unlike in most instructional design books, I also provide hints and tips to deliver your class effectively. Throughout this guide, you will practice and rehearse what you develop, so that when you teach your class or train via your Webinar for the first time, you will be ready.

Who Is the Kite Method For?

I have taught hundreds of people to successfully build Kites, in highly diverse contexts. Human resource professionals use the Kite Method to build employee skills; small business owners use it to create seminars that help convert prospects into customers. And "regular people" with passion and expertise in a particular subject use the Kite Method to teach adults in a wide variety of community situations.

Success Stories

1   A public library system used the Kite Method to develop training for hundreds of community members learning to use computers and electronic readers.

2   A one-person accounting firm used the Kite Method to develop and present a seminar entitled "Bookkeeping for Small Businesses" citywide, increasing his client base by 20 percent in three months.

3   A city police department successfully trained 250 supervisors and managers in supervisory skills using the Kite Method.

4   An individual between jobs learned to develop training using the Kite Method and was hired for a position that included instructional design.

5   Technology trainers in a major hospital used the Kite Method to improve mandatory training in electronic recordkeeping. Doctors reported that the training was now much more interesting, active, and beneficial.

About This Book

Although you can find a wide variety of books focusing on presentation skills in any bookstore, you will find few that teach non-experts to design courses for adults. This book closes that gap. It is colorful and skinny—for a reason. Although it integrates educational research, it is purposely brief and non-academic. Plus, it's small enough to fit into a briefcase.

I organized this book into four sections. In Part One you explore whether or not you need to spend the time and resources to develop a class. Part Two prepares you to build your Kite. You will notice that Part Three is by far the biggest part of the book because this is where you develop the "meat" of your class. Part Three provides step-by-step guidance to construct your Kite and includes templates, checklists, and worksheets to ensure that your Kite can withstand the toughest weather conditions. Part Four will help you launch your Kite.

This book provides the design tools you need to train both in a physical location and via a synchronous Webinar. Each is marked with an icon:

 Classroom Activities    Webinar Activities

I have purposefully included activities that will work with the simplest and least-expensive Webinar platforms, since not everyone has access to more sophisticated options. The activities provide a starting point for those with access to higher-end equipment.

This book focuses primarily on the needs of "all-in-one" trainers: individuals or small design committees who know a lot about their topic and plan to teach the class themselves. Although the Kite Method can be used to train individuals, it is most effective when used to design classes for groups of people.

Online Templates and Additional Resources

In this book, I have included the templates, checklists and worksheets you need to create a dynamic class or Webinar. I have also created a special part of my website just for you. By visiting www.guilamuir.com/kite-resources/ and using the password below, you can download every template, checklist, and worksheet in this book, plus additional resources. These will enable you to design class after class on any variety of topics.

Password (unique to readers of this guide): **Kiteresources** (case sensitive)

A Quick Guide to Kite Method Terms

Throughout this book, I'll be using the following terminology:

You, Trainer. The person designing and (usually) teaching the class.

Participant. The adult student.

Kite. Your class or learning experience. This can be a course, lesson, synchronous Webinar, seminar, workshop, module, unit of instruction, and so forth.

 Onsite class. A class that takes place in a physical location, such as a classroom, community center, conference room, etc.

 Synchronous Webinar. A live, online class, which enables a collection of people to learn the same things at the same time while not being in the same physical location.

Building the Kite. Creating your class using the Kite template with these four elements:
Frame: Purpose and Outcomes
Sail: Context
Sail: Body
Tail: Active Closure

Flying the Kite. Teaching your class.

My Learning Outcomes for You

By reading this book and doing the activities, you will be able to:

- Determine whether or not training is the best way for you to address performance problems in your workplace or community.
- Build the framework for an effective class.
- Create content, materials, and activities to bring your class alive.
- Powerfully and dynamically teach your class.
- Evaluate your class's impact.
- Use the Kite Method to design future classes of any length, on any subject, at any time.

So—let's get started!

PART TWO

Planning Your Kite

Ask the right questions if you're to find the right answers.
Vanessa Redgrave

Chapter 2

Before You Begin

Do You Even Need to Build a Kite?

Robert Mager famously said, "Almost every non-training tool … [is] faster and cheaper to implement than instruction. That's why we think of instruction, like surgery, as a last resort."[1]

Do you need to build a Kite? The sad truth is that many people spend countless hours designing gorgeous Kites, only to discover that their organizations lack the wind to fly them. To discover if building a Kite is really necessary, you need to carefully check the weather conditions first.

Because this book primarily focuses on class design and not on needs assessment, I've decided to provide only the simplest overview of the essential questions you should ask. Multiple books on the market will give you more in-depth instructions. (Many of these books are listed in the course design resource section, which starts on page 125.)

Here are the three essential questions you must be able to answer before starting to build your Kite:

1. What is the problem?
2. Is group training the only solution?
3. How will you know when the problem has been solved?

Three Examples

Using surveys, interviews, and questionnaires, staff in each of the organizations below asked stakeholders the essential three questions. Each organization then analyzed the answers carefully. Ultimately, they all made the decision to move ahead with training based on the answers they received, their budgets, and other forces unique to their organizations.

The organization highlighted in the Case Study asked the same questions and decided that training was not necessary. That organization chose to unroll other interventions that involved significantly less time and energy than training.

1. What is the problem?

Avoid the urge to build training because it seems like a good idea. What problem are you trying to solve?

Here are some real-life examples.

Who: Activity director, assisted-living complex
Problem: Residents don't know how to use e-mail to connect with family members.

Who: State Department of Revenue
Problem: An increased number of small business owners are calling because they're confused about how to file taxes under the new regulations.

Who: Global corporation selling high-end measurement equipment
Problem: New clients have returned equipment because they can't use it properly.

You can identify the problem by using surveys, interviews, and other available data. Often, what seems to be the problem initially morphs into something more tangible as you ask questions and explore further. You need to be able to state clearly the problem before moving to the next step.

2. Is group training the only solution? Do easier, cheaper, or better ways exist to fix the problem?

Often the problem is not a learning problem but one involving communication, interpersonal relationships, or leadership. Explore other options before deciding you need to build a Kite. You may solve the problem better, and save time, by considering some of these alternatives:

- Providing feedback through coaching or performance appraisals.
- Sending a memo.
- Tutoring using Skype or other teleconferencing program.
- Creating a blog or e-book.
- Providing better tools or equipment.
- Sending quickie how-tos via Twitter.
- Facilitating planning sessions.
- Undertaking disciplinary procedures for non-compliant employees.
- Developing checklists and other job aids.
- Introducing incentive systems, both monetary and non-monetary.
- Creating a newsletter.
- Initiating organizational change using focus groups and interviews.

Explore all alternatives to training first. Remember to think of training as the "intervention of last resort."

3. How will you know when the problem has been solved? What will have changed?

By visualizing what will have changed when the problem is solved, you clarify your desired end point. This helps you decide whether or not to build a Kite. It also helps focus your efforts and provides important evaluation criteria.

People in the examples above visualized their situations (once solved) in the following ways:

Who: Activity director, assisted-living complex
Problem: Residents don't know how to use e-mail to connect with family members.
What will have changed: Those residents who wish to send e-mails can do so relatively easily.

Who: State Department of Revenue
Problem: An increased number of small business owners are calling because they're confused about how to file taxes under the new regulations.
What will have changed: We receive 50 percent fewer calls about this issue.

Who: Global corporation selling high-end measurement equipment
Problem: New clients have returned equipment because they can't use it properly.
What will have changed: All clients can confidently perform the most necessary measurement actions immediately upon setting up the equipment in their factories.

CASE STUDY: Nightmare Meetings
No Kite Needed!

Who: City agency

Problem: Meetings are unproductive and too long.

What will have changed: Meetings are productive and rarely exceed one hour in length.

When a new director came into a city agency, she noticed that numerous meetings took place. She wondered if most of the meetings were necessary and productive.

The director asked employees to observe and provide verbal feedback to her about meetings. She also surveyed employees and clients online. The findings were very clear. Meetings were unproductive and too long. People had never really learned to facilitate and were simply replicating what they saw others do.

The director formed a small committee to review ways to improve meetings. Through reading a few books and articles, the group extracted best practices. One major suggestion was that staff develop and use meeting ground rules whenever leading a meeting.

Soon, most staff used ground rules. Using these did prevent and address the most time-wasting behaviors. However, using ground rules didn't significantly shorten meetings or make them productive enough for most people.

One employee's name kept appearing as someone whose meetings were highly productive. The director asked her to develop an "Elements of a Good Meeting" checklist. Soon, all meeting facilitators used the checklist. Meetings improved dramatically, and most took less than one hour.

This situation didn't need a group training program. The agency effectively used a "study group" intervention to identify an easy solution (the use of ground rules). It then used the subject matter expertise of just one employee to create a helpful checklist, avoiding the time and expense that group training would necessitate.

Ultimately, five other agency locations around the city used the "Elements of a Good Meeting" checklist. In a survey done three months later, the director found that employees actually met less frequently but had more productive meetings when they did meet.

If Building a Kite Is the Answer

Once you consider alternatives and have determined that training is the right way to address the problem, the Kite Method will help you tremendously.
Start out by making sure you can answer these questions:

1. *Who are the participants?* What are their characteristics, needs, anxieties, job titles, previous experiences, levels of expertise, etc.? Why are these the targeted participants? The more *specific* questions you can answer about your participants, the more powerful and focused your Kite will be.

2. *How long will your class be?* The amount of time you have in which to deliver the class will dramatically influence everything about it. If you don't know exactly, choose a time period NOW. You can always make changes in the future if necessary.

3. *Are you a content expert in the area for which you're building the Kite?* It's important that you know a lot about your subject. You don't have to know everything, but if you are a novice on this topic, you may want to work with at least one subject-matter expert. Don't try to learn about a topic at the same time you are building the Kite … you'll get overwhelmed.

4. *What form will the Kite take?* Will you develop classroom training, a seminar for the community, a Webinar? Will you deliver it via teleconference, DVD, streaming video? (I focus on onsite and synchronous Webinar training throughout this handbook, but the guidelines can be used for training in any medium.)

5. *Who will build and deliver the Kite?* Will you design and present the class on your own? Will you work with a small committee or an even larger group? Will you design the training and then pass it to someone else to train? (This book is primarily for those who develop and deliver training themselves, although others will find it useful.)

6. *Clarify: Will you present or train?* When Confucius declared the following, he was speaking of training:

> What I hear, I forget.
> What I see, I remember.
> What I do, I understand.

Presenting differs from training. Typically, presenting involves one-way communication; training is multi-directional and participatory. It builds skills. Although this book will help you develop a dynamic presentation, I wrote it specifically for those who want to build their participants' skills through participation and interaction.

Compare how a participant might experience the difference between a presentation and a training session.

Your role as a participant during a presentation called "Using Mylar to Create a Kite":

> Listen to someone tell you how to do it. Watch a slideshow about the necessary steps.

Your role as a participant during a training session called "Using Mylar to Create a Kite":

+ Review diagrams, pictures, slides, and written materials.

+ Write in a workbook.

+ Have someone verbally guide you through each step.

+ Share your frustrations and questions with the teacher and with other students.

- Actively get your hands on the materials you need. Fool around with them.
- Ask questions when you run into difficulties.
- Experiment and fail, then try it again.
- Receive helpful feedback and input.
- Go outside and try flying your kite, then make alterations if necessary.

How Adults Learn

As you set out to build your Kite, it's important to understand what adults need to learn effectively. Keep this information in mind both as you build your Kite and when you fly it.

Adults learn best when:

1. *They are actively involved in the learning.* Who wants to sit around passively, watching other people enjoy flying their kites? The fun part is in the doing. That's where learning occurs, too. Whether it's a Webinar or onsite class, make it active and participatory.

2. *Your material connects with participants' real-life experiences and emotions, whether in the past, present, or future.* The learning experience goes deeper when it hooks into something your participants know or feel.

    Past: New information has a better chance of sticking if you connect it with your participants' experiences, *particularly emotional ones.* What might be your participants' gut feelings or visceral memories? Connect your message to these, and it will go deep.

    Present: Focus on the participants' immediate needs. They'll learn better when your material helps them perform necessary skills, reduces anxiety, or offers solutions to relevant, real-life problems.

    Future: Focus on the participants' real concerns, anxieties, and hopes for the future. Emotion goes a long way in learning.

3. *You acknowledge and show that you care about each participant.* Whether you are teaching onsite or online, you need to show authentic interest in your participants. Ask a bit about them in pre-class conversations. Request photographs before online sessions.

Match names to faces. Share a bit about yourself. Model your belief that learning is a collaborative experience. Elicit suggestions from participants about how they might best learn.

Once you have determined if a Kite is really necessary and explored how adults learn best, you are ready to start building your Kite's framework.

PART THREE

Building Your Kite

We need structure or everything falls apart.
Jonah Lehrer

Building your Kite is creative and satisfying. In Part Three, you will build a strong, flexible frame by developing your class's purpose and outcomes. You will then fill that structure with your expertise and use activities to bring your class alive. Using the Kite Method ensures that your class has a logical flow that energizes and engages your participants from beginning to end.

Chapter 3

The Frame
Purpose and Outcomes

Overview

We've all seen those gorgeous kites flying on
sunny days. People feel happy just looking
at them. What does a kite need to fly so
gloriously? Its sail, usually made of bright fabric
stretched across a T-shaped framework, is the
kite's most eye-catching element. Yet that glorious
sail would remain slumped on the ground without
its underlying structure. To fly, a kite's frame must
be sturdy. The frame holds the entire kite together and
provides its shape.

LEARNING OUTCOMES

CLASS PURPOSE

In training design, the purpose and learning outcomes
make up the Kite's essential structure. Without this
framework, all you have is unorganized content. Many new course designers
make the mistake of gathering tons of data and information they want to
transmit without building their frame first. They end up with shapeless
piles of content lying on the floor and no clue about how to structure it
into something useable.

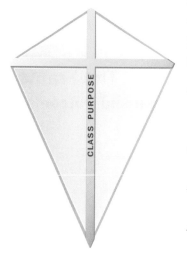

Purpose Statement

Your class's purpose statement acts as your Kite's vertical strut, or stick and is the first thing to develop. The purpose statement:

- Points your class directly at the problem you identified when you considered building a Kite.
- Helps keep **you** focused and on track as you develop the class.
- Serves as the basis for evaluation and accountability.
- Provides the essential structure for everything that follows.

The purpose statement should be succinct and simple. State in clear language *who* your audience is and *what* the topic is. Here are three examples:

- The purpose of this two-hour class is to help front-line supervisors write e-mails more clearly and concisely.
- The purpose of this seminar is to teach you how to use the Get Fit program.
- The purpose of this Webinar is to improve the presentation skills of accounting professionals.

Where to Start

The best way to develop your purpose statement is to determine the length of your class or Webinar. Then start with this bare-bones formula:

The purpose of this class is to:

(1) verb
(2) audience
(3) topic.

Note #2 and #3 are reversible—you can put either first.

Your purpose statement will sound simple, maybe even a little blunt. State it in "real-people" language. Don't get fancy or academic sounding, and use short words.

Your choice of verb is important. Do you want to *orient* your participants to something? Or do you want to *teach* them? Do you want to *introduce* them to something, or do you want to *train* them to do something?

Play around with different verbs and see which ones feel right for your allotted time. It will take less time to orient the participants to something than to train them to do something. Choose a verb that you can actually do in the time allotted for your class.

Worksheet: Purpose Statement #1

Try it out! Think of a topic you want to develop into a class. Write it here, using this formula: *"The purpose of this (how long?) class is to (verb) (who) (what)."*

The purpose of this _____ (how long?) class is to

_____
(verb)

_____
(who)

_____
(what)

Once you identify who the participants are, you can just substitute "you" for the "who." This personalizes the statement and helps you connect to your participants.

Here are several examples:

- The purpose of this two-hour class is to help **you** write e-mails more clearly and concisely.

- The purpose of this seminar is to teach **you** how to use the Get Fit program.

- The purpose of this Webinar is to improve **your** presentation skills.

Picture your audience in your head as you write your purpose statement again. Is this the right purpose for this group of people?

The purpose of this _____ (how long?) class is to

_____
(verb)

you _____
(what)

What's in It for *Them?*

Once you have developed your basic purpose statement using the formula above, you can highlight its benefits to the participants. Doing so helps to persuade participants of the importance and relevance of your topic to their lives. It can work as a powerful incentive for them to engage just seconds into your class.

Compare these purpose statements, written with the benefits in mind, to the examples on page 23.

- ◆ The purpose of this two-hour class is to help you communicate more effectively by writing clear and concise e-mails.

- ◆ The purpose of this seminar is to teach you tips and techniques to get the most out of the Get Fit program.

- ◆ The purpose of this Webinar is to increase your comfort and confidence as a presenter.

Worksheet: Purpose Statement #2

Try re-writing your class purpose. Insert the benefit to your participants:

The purpose of this _____ (how long?) class is to:

_____

_____

_____

_____

Whether you decide to focus on the benefits or to keep it simple, remember always to start with the simplest statement, using the formula:

The purpose of this class is to:
    (1) verb
    (2) audience
    (3) topic.

That's it—you have created half your Kite's framework. Let's complete it!

Learning Outcomes

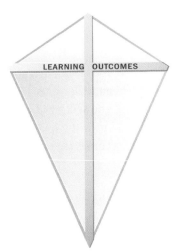

Begin with the end in mind.
Peter Senge

The learning outcomes act as your Kite's horizontal strut or stick. Learning outcomes are exceedingly important. They not only complete the framework; they also impact everything you do in developing the rest of your Kite. Learning outcomes determine:

- Which specific content and learning activities you will include.

- How you will evaluate the success and effectiveness of your Kite's flight.

I choose to use the term "learning outcome" instead of "goal" or "objective" because the word "outcome" indicates *what will have changed* for your participants by the end of the class. A learning outcome is not your open-ended hope, wish, or goal for the class. Instead, it concretely describes what participants will be able to do by the end of your class that they couldn't do before.

You need to develop learning outcomes for your class immediately after developing the class's purpose.

What Are Learning Outcomes?

Learning outcomes are your promises or guarantees of what the participants will be able to **do** by the end of your class. Learning outcomes are directly connected to your class's purpose, which points directly at the problem you exposed when trying to find out if building a Kite was necessary in the first place.

Good learning outcomes are:

- Based on *who* your participants are.
- Targeted at the problem you identified.
- Specific and concise.
- Demonstrable by the participants *before* they leave the classroom or Webinar.

Things to Consider When Developing Learning Outcomes

THE LENGTH OF YOUR CLASS

Your class's length is a great informer. It will help you decide exactly what content can and cannot be included. Don't be like the designer who promises, "By the end of this thirty-minute training, you will be able to solve the problem of world hunger." It is essential to know the length of your proposed class before developing the learning outcomes so that your participants can actually achieve them in that timeframe.

NECESSARY EQUIPMENT AND MATERIALS

Make sure that you have everything you need to enable participants to DO what you are promising they will be able to do. For example, if you guarantee that your participants will be able to demonstrate five shortcuts using Microsoft Word, make sure they can do so using a computer during class.

How to Develop Your Learning Outcomes

1. BRAINSTORM CONTENT

The first step is to brainstorm potential content. To do this, use a pen and paper, not a computer. Use the worksheet on the following page.

Worksheet: Brainstorming Content

Ask yourself, "If I had *all the time in the world* to teach *every aspect of this topic*, what would I include?" Give yourself only ten minutes to brainstorm ALL the content you can possibly think of that might relate to your proposed training. Try to list thirty items without judging or stopping to think about the worthiness of each element. Just keep slapping down ideas without letting your pen leave the page.

Brainstorm at least **30** potential pieces of information in the time allotted. **DON'T stop to judge or analyze anything you've written.**

1. _____

2. _____

3. _____

4. _____

5. _____

6. _____

7. _____

8. _____

9. _____

10. _____

11. _____

12. _____

13. _____

14. _____

15. _____

16. _____

17. _____

18. _____

19. _____

20. _____

21. _____

22. _____

23. _____

24. _____

25. _____

26. _____

27. _____

28. _____

29. _____

30. _____

2. CREATE CONTENT CLUMPS

Once you have brainstormed content, go back and circle the absolute "must-know" pieces of content. Keep your proposed participants in mind. What do they want? What do they need? (How do you know this?)

To determine the "must-knows," ask yourself, "If this piece of content were missing, would my class be a complete flop?" Consider your purpose statement and your participants' level of knowledge. Ask yourself if smaller pieces can be put together under one larger umbrella. Draw lines to show which smaller areas can be pulled together into one larger content clump.

As you do so, ask yourself, "Is this too much content for the time allotted?" Listen to your gut. If it feels like too much content, it probably is. You may have to leave some content out or provide more time for the class.

Although there is no steadfast rule about how many content clumps you should have for specific lengths of training, here are some guidelines you might find helpful:

If your class is:

Up to one hour long: Create 1-2 content clumps
3-4 hours long: Create 2-5 content clumps
All day long: Create 4-6 content clumps

Remember, these times are estimations based on experience. There are always exceptions, as in some one-day training sessions with only three large clumps of content. It is usually best to have fewer, larger content clumps than many small ones.

You will now transform these content clumps into the most exciting structural element of the Kite: learning outcomes. Once you determine your learning outcomes, developing the rest of the Kite is easy!

3. TRANSFORM YOUR "MUST-KNOW" CONCEPTS INTO LEARNING OUTCOMES

Look at one of your content clumps (this could be one that has many parts to it). Ask yourself this question: "How would I *know* that my participants know this by the end of the session? What would I *see* or *hear* that would prove they know this?" Think about it.

Always start your outcome statements with words like these: *"By the end of this session, participants will be able to ..."*

Then use an action word such as:

- navigate
- perform
- describe
- name
- list
- match
- select
- define
- demonstrate (if the necessary equipment is present)

Is the session longer, or the content more complex? Maybe your participants could:

- give examples
- explain why
- summarize
- estimate
- prepare
- produce
- use
- teach
- organize

To Develop a Learning Outcome

Ask yourself, "How would I **know** that my participants know this by the end of the session? What would I **see** or **hear** that would prove they know this?"

Here's an example from a real-life, two-hour class on writing effective e-mails:

This trainer's purpose: *"The purpose of this two-hour class is to help you communicate more effectively by writing clear and concise e-mails."*

By looking at her circled content clumps, this trainer saw three major topic areas and some other, scattered pieces that could probably fit into each of those larger areas. She turned these clumps into these learning outcomes:

By the end of this session, you will be able to:

1. Explain the three most important e-mail etiquette rules.

2. Correct basic punctuation in several e-mails and be able to describe the rules used.

3. Compose and send an e-mail that integrates these etiquette and punctuation rules.

To develop these learning outcomes, she asked herself for each one, "Would I be able to see or hear the participants do this?" She finalized the outcomes only when she was sure that she'd be able to do so in her class's allotted time.

Use the worksheet below to transform your content clumps into learning outcomes.

Worksheet: Transforming Your Content Clumps into Learning Outcomes

What is the purpose of your class? (See page 22.)

The purpose of this class is to:

_____

_____

_____

Transform the concept(s) you circled on page 27 into learning outcomes.

As a result of this (how long?) _____class, participants will be able to:

1.
_____

2.
_____

Depending on the length of your session, you may not need any more outcomes. What do you think?

3.
_____

4.
_____

Making Your Learning Outcomes Even Better

By using a number in your learning outcomes, you tighten them up and make them more specific. Compare the following:

By the end of this three-hour training, you'll be able to describe ...
+ a CCTV system.
+ the four components of a CCTV system.

By the end of this two-hour training, you'll be able to demonstrate ...
+ effective presentation techniques.
+ at least five effective presentation techniques.

Which do you think best clarifies what the participants are expected to learn? In each case, the second example informs participants exactly what they will be able to do as a result of the class.

You also make your own design job easier when you quantify a learning outcome. Providing a number helps you apply the "acid test" ("must-know" vs. "nice-to-know") to all the content in your head, enabling you to pluck out and use only the most important points.

Using the previous worksheet, stick a number into at least one of the learning outcomes you developed. Keep your class's allotted time in mind. See how including a number improves the outcome while simplifying your job as the Kite builder!

By figuring out your learning outcomes early in the process, it becomes very clear what your content (and even some of your activities) should be. You've completed the most challenging step of creating your Kite.

Preview

Your learning outcomes play an essential role in the next piece of the Kite you'll design, its Context.

Rehearse Your Learning Outcomes Aloud

Learning outcomes play an important role both to you and to your participants. By stating learning outcomes aloud to yourself *before* the class, you:

+ Clarify your own direction.

- Determine the benchmarks you want participants to achieve, allowing you to evaluate learning at the end of the class.

Stating the learning outcomes aloud *during* the class has a positive psychological effect on your participants. By doing so, you

- Clarify your expectations for their performance.
- Let them know what to expect.
- Focus their brains in the right direction.

Worksheet: Purpose and Learning Outcomes Try It Out.

Transfer your class's Purpose and Learning Outcomes (page 30) here. Don't forget to quantify them where possible. This becomes your script.

The purpose of this class is to: _____

As a result of this (how long?) _____class, you will be able to:

1. _____

2. _____

3. _____

Now, rehearse! Here are the steps:

- Stand up
- Hold this script in your left hand.
- Clearly state your purpose and learning outcomes out loud.
- Try stating them again so that they sound less stilted. Remember, these are your promises, or guarantees, of what the participants will gain from the session. By stating your purpose and learning outcomes out loud, you are making a concrete commitment to your participants.
- Repeat until your purpose and learning outcomes flow naturally, in a conversational style.

Additional Resources on Learning Outcomes

What is a Learning Outcome?

An outcome is a statement of what each participant will be able to **do** as a result of the training session.

Participants should be able to demonstrate the learning outcome **before** they walk out of the session.

Begin each outcome with some variation of the words: *"As a result of this session, you'll be able to …"*

Before Developing an Outcome	Ask yourself: In a perfect world, what would the participants *know* by the end of my session? Brainstorm all potential items.
Develop the Outcome	Ask yourself:
	◆ What are the *essential "must-knows"* from my list? (Other issues may fit into these broader categories.)
	◆ How would I *know* that the participants know these things by the end of the training? What would I *see or hear* that would prove they know this?
	Then start the outcome statement with these words:
	"By the end of this session, participants will be able to ..."
	Then use an action word. (See next page.)
Use the Outcome to Evaluate How Well They Got It	At the end of the class, evaluate how successful you were in teaching your subject by asking: *Can the participants prove that they know in a visible or audible way?*

Action Words for Your Learning Outcomes

Some verbs are easier to demonstrate; others verbs demand deeper cognitive action and more time to accomplish. In choosing your verb, it's important that you weigh the:

- Complexity of the content
- Length of the class
- Existing level of participant knowledge

For a short (two-hour) session, most likely you will want participants to:

- navigate
- perform
- describe
- name
- list
- match
- select
- define
- demonstrate (if necessary equipment is present)

For a longer or more cognitively demanding class, you will want to choose a verb that requires a deeper level of understanding, such as:

- give examples
- explain why
- summarize
- estimate
- prepare
- produce
- use
- teach
- organize

Remember—you will TEST to see if the participants can DO what you promised they would—*before* they walk out of the class.

Note

The verbs "identify," "recognize," "understand," and "learn" are not on either list. Why?

Answer: No one can **see or hear** these actions since they take place internally. Instead, use actions that can be seen or heard, such as "point to," "pick up," "draw a circle around," and so forth.

Test Yourself!
Is This a Good Learning Outcome?

Circle the number of each *"No Good"* learning outcome. Jot down the reason(s) you made that decision.

As a result of this session, participants will be able to ...

1. Know different kinds of mosquito-borne diseases.

2. List characteristics of a domestic violence situation.

3. List five characteristics most typical of a domestic violence situation.

4. Understand how to take a shower.

5. Take a shower. *(Class takes place in an open field.)*

6. In order, describe the five most important things that occur from the time a 911 call is received to the time the patrol car responds.

7. Without notes, explain at least five features of the Get Fit program.

8. Learn how to make a chocolate-marble cake.

9. In order, list the ten steps necessary to make a chocolate-marble cake.

10. Make a chocolate-marble cake. *(Three-hour class.)*

(See answers, next page.)

Answers to Test Yourself!

Is This a Good Learning Outcome?

As a result of this session, participants will be able to ...

1. Know different kinds of mosquito-borne diseases.

   NO GOOD! Reason: As a trainer, would you be able to see or hear if your participants "know" this? Change the verb to "name," "describe" or "explain," stick in a number, and make it more specific: "Participants will be able to name and describe the three primary types of mosquito-borne diseases found in tropical climates."

2. List characteristics of a domestic violence situation.

   This one is barely OK. It's pretty vague. The next one, #3, is much better. Why?

3. List five characteristics most typical of a domestic violence situation.

   This learning outcome is more specific, improving it tremendously. It includes a number and the words "most typical." When you can quantify (provide a number to) a learning outcome, you make your own work as a designer easier. You only have to cover these five things.

   By providing a number, you also clarify your expectations to the participants—they know they are expected to list five characteristics, (not just "some").

   Words like "most typical," "essential," "most important," "primary," etc. improve your learning outcome by making it more specific.

4. Understand how to take a shower.

   NO GOOD! Reason: You can't *see* or *hear* "understand." What verb would make this better? Can you supply a number to make it more specific?

5. Take a shower. (Class takes place in an open field.)

   NO GOOD! Reason: You don't have the necessary equipment.

6. In order, describe the five most important things that occur from the time a 911 call is received to the time the patrol car responds.

   GOOD! Reason: It's specific and doable.

7. Without notes, explain at least five features of the Get Fit program.

   GOOD! Reason: It's specific and doable and includes the condition "without notes," making it more specific.

8. Learn how to make a chocolate-marble cake.

NO GOOD! Reason: You can't *see* or *hear* "learn." What verb would make this better?

9. In order, list the ten steps necessary to make a chocolate-marble cake.

GOOD! Reason: It's specific and doable.

10. Make a chocolate-marble cake. (*Three-hour class.*)

GOOD! Reason: It's specific and doable in the time allotted. And you have a delicious reward!

CHAPTER 3
The Frame: Purpose and Outcomes

Summary

1. You'll never fly a Kite if it doesn't have a frame. Always develop your purpose statement and learning outcomes first.

2. Your purpose statement points your class directly at the problem you uncovered when you assessed if you needed to build a Kite.

3. Your learning outcomes are statements of what the participants will be able to *do* by the end of the class. You must be able to *see* or *hear* the learning outcomes when your participants achieve them. They must be achievable in your allotted class time.

To download the worksheets and resources you used in this chapter, go to www.guilamuir.com/kite-resources/ and enter your special password (**Kiteresources**).

Now that you have successfully built your frame, you are ready to craft the sail—the most visible and dynamic part of your Kite.

Chapter 4

The Sail
Context

The material that the kite's sail is made from directly affects how the kite will fly.
Mackite.com

Overview

The next step in building a kite is to stretch material, called the sail, over the frame. When you stretch the material over the structure, you give your kite its shape. It actually starts *looking* like a kite.

Think of the amazing color combinations and designs you've seen in kites. Their sails are where they show off their beauty and uniqueness. It's the same for any class you develop using the Kite Method. The choices you make to build your sail differentiate your class from all others, even those on the same topic or subject.

There are two parts of the sail: the context and the body. The context readies your participants to learn, and the body is where instruction takes place. The context and the body are seamlessly stitched together. In Chapters 4 and 5, you will complete your sail by building both these parts.

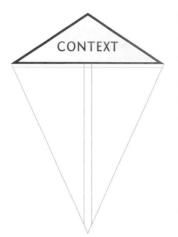

Context

The context section prepares your participants' brains for the learning experience ahead. By setting the context, you create a safe, engaging, and interesting place to learn.

The context section has four segments:

1. Hook

2. Trainer and participant introductions

3. Information about the class

4. Transition

(Note: You will include your class's purpose and learning outcomes, which you created in the previous chapter, in the final design of your context. See page 58, Set Your Context Template.)

You may find it easiest to create the four segments in the order listed here. However, you don't need to. You may choose to skip the context section for now and move on to designing your Kite's body (Chapter 5).

> No matter which part of your Kite you decide to design next, make sure you have created your purpose and outcomes first. Since these comprise the Kite's frame, you need them in place before you can build any other part of your Kite

1. Crafting an Attention-getting Hook

Test Yourself! Is there anything wrong with the following scenarios?
Check "yes" or "no."

1. Helen begins her Webinar by introducing herself and telling the participants at some length how happy she is to be with them. She then launches into her content.

Yes ☐   No ☐

2. Bill kicks off his onsite training session by explaining where the bathrooms and telephones are. He then asks people to go around the room and introduce themselves.

Yes ☐   No ☐

The correct answer to both is **yes!** There is something wrong with both scenarios. Neither Helen nor Bob is using a Hook. They have squandered their one-time-only opportunity to *immediately* get their participants involved. Inadvertently, they have both weakened their class's effectiveness.

I just used the questions above to hook you, my reader. A Hook is an umbrella statement, activity, or question that provides a conceptual link between the learner's existing knowledge and new information. By using a Hook, you engage your participants immediately.

Below, I provide you with five great ideas for Hooks. All five will work in both onsite and online environments. But first, let's explore what a Hook is and is not.

What a Hook is NOT:

- *Fluff.* Don't make the mistake of thinking that a Hook is unimportant and can be left out. It helps open the participants' brains to learning new things.

- *Lengthy.* A Hook is typically not a full-blown exercise, energizer, or icebreaker.

- *A pre-test.* Don't use a Hook to identify the "smartest guys in the room."

- *A vacuous way to fill those nervous first moments of a training session when you feel least confident.* A Hook has a definite role. Don't waste the precious first moments of a class with comments about the weather or other unrelated issues.

What a Hook IS:

- *Relatively short.* Although there is no actual rule about length, the Hook should serve its purpose concisely.

- *Connected to the session's topic or purpose.* Although anything can serve as a Hook, spend some creative thought making solid connection between the Hook and your purpose. Don't lob out a meaningless joke just to get laughs.

- *Connected to who your participants are.* You must know your audience's concerns. The best Hooks relate to their real experiences, either past or present.

- *Emotional, even if only mildly so.* Adults become engaged through their emotions. Good Hooks incite almost any kind of emotion, including laughter, groans of recognition, anxiety, or curiosity.

- *Inclusive.* Use a Hook that all the participants can relate to. Again, the best Hooks elicit the past knowledge, emotions, and/ or experiences of most people in your audience.

Developing a Hook that includes these attributes takes careful preparation on your part. However, your Hook will suffer if any of these attributes is left out. So will your participants' interest and involvement.

Five Dynamite Hooks

You can use literally anything as a Hook. Trainers have used visual aids, such as short videos or toys from the local Dollar Store. They have used riddles, music, anecdotes, yoga stretches, and many more ways to immediately engage their participants.

The five Hooks I outline here have proven to work with a bang every time.

1. REAL-LIFE QUESTIONS

 Have you ever been immediately drawn into a training session because the instructor asked a question that intrigued, angered, or excited you?

With that question, I've just modeled one of the easiest types of Hook to create: the real-life question. To ensure that your real-life question effectively hooks your participants, make sure you know enough about your audience to use topics that resonate with them. Also, as in all Hooks, ensure that your questions both integrate and elicit an emotional response.

In a Webinar, ask questions both verbally and visually. Use either the Raise Hands or the Polling tool.

Guidelines:

- Always ask a *minimum* of two questions. You need more than one to get your participants' brains moving in the direction of your training session.

- Create your questions so that nearly everyone will respond in the same way.

- Make it clear that you expect a physical response, such as standing up or raising hands. Don't move to your next question until everyone responds.

Here's an example from a training session on public speaking:

"Please raise your hands if you've ever gotten a queasy stomach, sweaty hands, or racing heart before speaking in public. (Look around; see the hands.)

"Please lower your hands if you've feared 'spacing out' or going blank in front of an audience.

"One last question—please raise your hands if you want to be the best speaker you can be.

"This training will help you achieve that goal. You can put your hands down now. Thank you!"

Here are some single-question examples, each used for different training sessions. See if you can guess the training topics:

"How many of you get so frustrated with your computer sometimes that you'd like to put your fist right through that screen?"

"Raise your hands if you've ever participated in a nightmare meeting."

"Raise your hands if you've ever hit your boiling point around kids—even if you don't have any!"

Alternate Idea:

Start your questions with the following:

"How many of you would NOT be willing to …?" (Remember, your goal is to get everyone's hand up. Asking in the negative may be more provocative and participatory than asking in the positive.)

2. "DID YOU KNOW?" (Provocative Fact or Statistic)

The world is full of provocative statistics you can use to hook your participants. Just keep your eyes out as you read blogs, newspapers, and articles. With a little thought, you can usually make the most unrelated statistic relevant to your class and its participants.

Guidelines:

+ Turn a provocative fact into a Hook simply by prefacing it with the words "did you know?"

+ Make sure your data is correct.

+ Make sure the fact will elicit emotion, even if slight.

+ Consider combining your fact or statistic with another Hook, such as a real-life question or a think-back.

Real-life Example

"Did you know … that Delta Airlines recently saved $210,000 a year simply by removing one strawberry from salads served in First Class? One little strawberry was removed, and passengers didn't even notice it. Big results can be achieved by little changes. Today, we'll talk about how little changes in your thoughts and attitudes can have big results in your own life." *(Thanks to Teri Lester, Sno-Isle Libraries, Washington)*

Here are three other examples, used in actual classes:

1. "Did you know that in one second …

- ◆ A telephone signal can travel one hundred thousand miles?
- ◆ A hummingbird beats its wings seventy times?
- ◆ And, guess what, eight million of your blood cells die?

A lot can happen in one second. This session will give you the tools to ensure that every second you spend with a stroke victim will increase his or her chance of a full recovery."

2. "Did you know that Generation Xers have watched twenty-three thousand hours of television by the time they are twenty years old? They also believe they have a better chance of seeing a UFO in their lifetime than a Social Security check. In this workshop, we'll see how generational differences in the workplace affect all of us."

3. "Before the rule, more than fifty people here were dying in trenches every year. When you get killed in a cave-in, it's not an easy way to go. You're literally crushed to death under the weight of the soil. Soil weighs approximately three thousand pounds per cubic yard. Nobody deserves to go to work and die that way."

You can also use the Internet to find relevant, provocative data. However, be sure to check its accuracy before using it as a part of your Hook.

3. THINK-BACK

The Think-back Hook is extremely powerful because it conjures visual images in each participant's brain. In fact, Think-back is one of the most evocative and effective Hooks you can use.

Ask the participants to recall an experience that had emotional meaning for them and that is relevant to the topic. You can request that they close their eyes (or cover them) for an even more evocative experience.

Example:

> "Picture yourself on the first day at your job. See yourself walking through the door that morning. Remember your thoughts and feelings as you met the people in your office for the first time. What worries did you carry in the door with you? What did you feel confident about? What did you want to know? … Please open your eyes.
>
> "Your new employees are experiencing those same emotions as they arrive. Let's focus on some ways to orient and train them effectively."

In a Webinar, give instructions verbally and visually. Make it clear that you expect the participants to do the exercise even if you can't see them. Then ask for responses using the Group Chat tool or microphones.

4. RIGHT FOOT

In this exercise, participants experience something that is actually impossible. You use that experience to highlight the possibilities of what they will learn in your session.

Tell participants to sit with both feet on the floor. Then say, "Lift your right foot and make clockwise circles." Once they do this, say "Continue. Now, raise your right hand and draw the number '6' in the air."

Everyone's foot will change direction.

Ask, "Is it impossible to do this?" The answer is yes. Say, "What we're talking about today may seem impossible at first—but you will see that it is very possible and achievable!"

You could also ask, "What would make this exercise doable?" Encourage experimentation. Participants will discover alternative ways to do the exercise. These include using their left hands to draw the "6," drawing another number, or any range of alternatives.

Give instructions verbally and visually. Make it clear that you expect the participants to do the exercise even if you can't see them. Use the chat box or microphones for reactions.

Say, "[Subject] is not impossible. This session will provide all the tips you need to make it as easy as you just made this seemingly impossible exercise."

Real-life Example of "Right Foot" Hook

Run the activity as described above. Then ask, "Why can't even the most accomplished multi-tasker do this?

"While many of us feel that we can multi-task, brain research tells us that our brains can pay attention only to a finite number of tasks at any one time. What we call 'multi-tasking' is simply dividing our concentration into smaller and smaller chunks. As a result, we spend more time trying to 'get back on task.' We actually accomplish less.

"In today's class, we will learn techniques that will allow you to accomplish more. You will also develop work habits that will allow you to concentrate on the project at hand." *(Thanks to Scott Wuerch, Royal Credit Union, Wisc.)*

5. QUICKIE QUIZ

A three-question quiz is a great way to kick off a training session, whether onsite or online.

Guidelines:

- The quiz is **not** a way to assess who knows more than others. Instead, it is a way of "turning on the brain."
- The quiz should include at least one amusing question or, at the least, be intriguing enough to elicit a "wow, I didn't know that!" response.

Provide each participant with a half-page paper quiz, facedown. Say something mock-serious such as, "I wanted to check your knowledge before we got started today, so we're going to start with a pop quiz. At the signal, please begin. You have thirty seconds to complete the quiz."

Give the signal. When thirty seconds have passed, say, "Pencils up!" Then go through the quiz, having participants respond to the answers.

Use the Polling function.

Here are two real-life examples of a quickie quiz.

Interactive Training: True or False?

1. T   F   Lectures kill.

2. T   F   Lots of games—especially those that involve physical contact, deep personal sharing, and interpretive dance—are essential for good training.

3. T   F   A "Hook" is an essential component of adult education.

(Note: It's interesting that most participants who take this quickie quiz answer the first question "true." This provides a great opportunity to inform them that no one has ever *actually* died from listening to a lecture. However, it's essential to use active training techniques to keep people engaged!)

The Library Quiz: Which Has More?

(Circle your answer.)

1. Establishments in the United States

McDonalds   Public libraries

2. Money spent on it in the US each year

Buying candy   Supporting public libraries

3. Attendance each year

Movie theaters   Libraries

(Answers: #1: Public libraries; #2: Buying candy, by twice as much; #3: Libraries, by three times as much.)

Source: Quotable Facts about America's Libraries 2010, American Library Association)

Although you designed your purpose first, you will kick off the class with the Hook.

"Combo Plate" Hooks

Often, the best Hooks are a combination of two types. For example, this Hook combines a real-life question Hook with a provocative fact:

> "Raise your hands if you know someone who has or had cancer.
>
> "Keep your hands raised if you fervently wish we could cure cancer in our lifetimes.
>
> "Please lower your hands if you want to learn tools and techniques to support a loved one throughout his or her journey with cancer.
>
> "Did you know? The truth is that, statistically, [number] percent of the [number] of us in this room today will die from cancer in the next ten years."

Hooks involve your participants from the get-go. They are an essential part of Kite design and will ensure that your Kite lifts powerfully into the air. Try creating a couple of Hooks using the following worksheet.

Worksheet: My Hook

The purpose of my class is to (from pages 23—24):

_____

_____

_____

A couple of Hooks I could try:

1. _____

_____

_____

_____

2. _____

_____

_____

_____

3. _____

_____

_____

_____

Note: Make sure there is a rational link between your purpose and your Hook. Massage your Hook until it truly leads to the purpose.

Now that you've designed some potential Hooks (and have your ears and eyes out for more Hooks you could use), let's take a look at how to effectively introduce yourself to your class.

2. Ensuring Introductions Add Value

Overview

Once you have hooked the participants, it's time for introductions. Introductions are important because they forge a connection between you and the participants, as well as among the participants themselves. By including introductions, you help to build a sense of community. You also build your own credibility and address the unspoken question: "Why is *this* person teaching our class?"

The Kite Method flies in the face of conventional wisdom because the Hook *precedes* the introductions. Your Hook engages your participants. Introductions deepen their commitment to your class.

Trainer Introduction

Let's look at how you typically introduce yourself. Do you follow your name with your professional title? Although you worked hard for that title, it often means little to class participants. Your title can even turn participants off because it sounds like industry jargon.

Compare the three examples below. Which statement in each pair actually says what the person does? Which statement is more compelling?

"I'm a recreation division manager" *OR*
"I turn recreation staff into leaders."

"I'm a reference librarian" *OR*
"I can help you find the answers to all your questions."

"I'm a youth development program coordinator" *OR*
"I empower youth."

To give a dynamic introduction,

- ◆ Focus on the **results** and **benefits** of what you do.
- ◆ Think of yourself as a *solution provider*, not a service provider.
- ◆ Focus your message on the people that you help.

Here are more examples. As before, the second choice is better.

"I work for Puget Sound Energy" OR
"I help keep your electricity bills low."

"I'm a financial consultant" OR
"I help people figure out how to save money."

"I'm a career coach" OR
"I help people turn their passions into viable careers."

Once you create an introduction that conveys how you help others, you can follow it up with your professional credentials, years of experience, education, and other details that build your credibility. Because you have already hooked your participants, they will more easily absorb these facts. They will be more open to your expertise. You will build your credibility painlessly.

Give it a try! Use this worksheet to develop a compelling introduction.

Worksheet: My Introduction

Write an introduction that:

- ◆ focuses on the results and benefits of what you do
- ◆ builds your credibility
- ◆ keeps your audience in mind

Remember—often, your professional title will NOT come first.

_____

_____

_____

_____

_____

_____

_____

_____

_____

_____

_____

Value-added Participant Introductions

Participant introductions, though an extremely important part of your Kite's context, should come after the trainer introduction. In fact, they should also follow the class's purpose and learning outcomes. The participants need to know what to expect from the class and who you are first. This clarity increases their comfort and goes a long way toward preventing turbulence later.

In the worst situations, participant introductions can take a lot of time and cause a training session to lose focus. You must structure this important piece of your session so that:

- Participants feel honored, welcome, and engaged
- Participants offer something of themselves
- The introductions flow swiftly and smoothly
- Introductions add value to the context section instead of causing it to lose focus.

How to Achieve Value-added Participant Introductions

 1. Provide a visual of what specific information participants should include in their introductions. This can be written on the flipchart or on a slide. DON'T just ask for their names—make this active!

Examples:

    a. Your name and job
       One thing that you enjoy most about your work

    b. Your name
       One question you have about [topic of session]

2. Model how to do it yourself. Make it short and concise. The chances are high that if you model a short intro, participants will take your lead. Make it clear that this segment will move quickly.

3. Tell the participants that you will call on each person to introduce him- or herself.

4. Keep it fast!

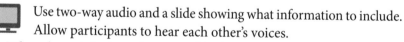
Use two-way audio and a slide showing what information to include. Allow participants to hear each other's voices.

When done right, introductions of both you and your participants help develop your class's sense of community. They help to boost interaction while keeping an energetic pace.

You've learned how to add value to your class by strategically introducing yourself and your participants. Next, let's explore the information you need to provide to ensure that your participants remain engaged and eager to learn.

3. Providing Essential Information about the Class

Your participants need to know what is expected of them during the class. They also need to know other information that will help them get the most out of the class. That's what the info section is all about.

Your info section, sometimes called "housekeeping," follows the Hook and introductions. Why? Because, although this information is important, it can drain energy from the training if it's delivered before the participants get engaged and active.

The more concise and necessary the information, the better. Here's the information you'll need to provide.

BEHAVIORAL EXPECTATIONS

 Set clear expectations for your participants' behavior during the class. By doing this early, you will prevent turbulence later. With a few exceptions, your expectations for both onsite classes and Webinars are probably similar. Your expectations could involve:

- Use of cell phones and electronic devices during class
- How you will deal with questions and comments
- Participant involvement during the session
- Timing of breaks
- Mute or unmute phones
- Protocol for questions

State your expectations. In an online environment, also show them on a slide.

LOGISTICAL INFORMATION

This section may also include some or all of the following information.

- Emergency procedures, exits, etc.
- Overview of the agenda
- Clarification of how long the breaks are and when they will occur
- Expectations for questions (will you welcome them throughout the session or only at the end of segments?)
- Parking information
- Information specific to the training (e.g., how it fits into a larger organizational structure, if the session is part of a sequence, political or financial realities that made the training necessary, etc.)

Worksheet: Expectations and Logistics Info

Think it through.

What information will you provide?

Behavioral Expectations	Logistical Information

You've decided the essential information your participants must know. Next, let's prepare to kick off the class by creating a simple transition.

4. Creating a Strong Transition

This tiny but important segment is key to moving smoothly from the context portion of the Kite into its body. After providing your behavioral expectations and other information about the training, simply build in a statement like one of these:

> "So, let's get started!"
> "Let's get the ball rolling."
> "Let's kick it off."

A smooth transition makes you look professional. It also prepares your participants to receive new input.

You are now ready to put your context piece together. Use the information you've generated so far to complete and present the template on the following pages.

Template: Set Your Context

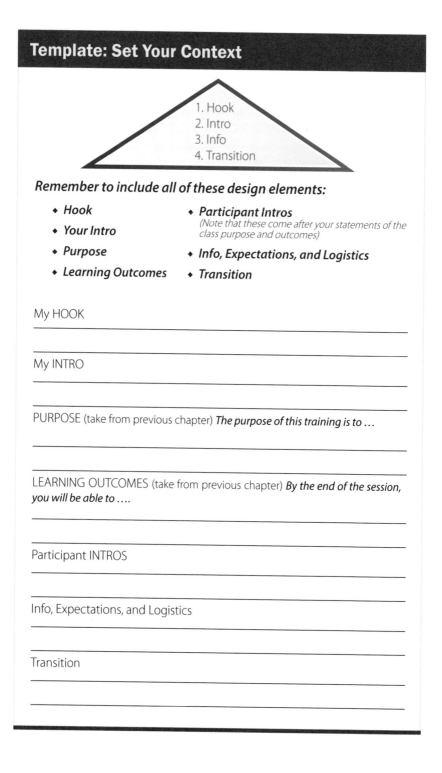

1. Hook
2. Intro
3. Info
4. Transition

Remember to include all of these design elements:

- ◆ **Hook**
- ◆ **Your Intro**
- ◆ **Purpose**
- ◆ **Learning Outcomes**

- ◆ **Participant Intros**
  (Note that these come after your statements of the class purpose and outcomes)
- ◆ **Info, Expectations, and Logistics**
- ◆ **Transition**

My HOOK

_____

_____

My INTRO

_____

_____

PURPOSE (take from previous chapter) *The purpose of this training is to …*

_____

_____

LEARNING OUTCOMES (take from previous chapter) *By the end of the session, you will be able to ….*

_____

_____

Participant INTROS

_____

_____

Info, Expectations, and Logistics

_____

_____

Transition

_____

_____

Exercise: Practice Your Context!

Picture yourself in the classroom or in front of your computer, ready to deliver your class for the first time. Do you feel unmoored, like a kite without a string? Or do you feel focused, soaring, and powerful?

The first few minutes of your class are extremely important because they determine whether you grab your participants' attention and interest, or squander it. The only way to ensure that you successfully engage your participants is to practice the context section several times, out loud. Here's how.

Get Ready!

- ◆ Stand up.
- ◆ Go to a full-length mirror (if possible) and stand in front of it.
- ◆ Plant your feet straight ahead. Look yourself in the eye. Smile.

Go!

- ◆ Hold your completed context template (page 58) in your left hand.
- ◆ Use this template as a script. Making as much eye contact with your mirror reflection as possible,
    - ◆ *Hook* your participants.
    - ◆ *Introduce* yourself.
    - ◆ *State* your purpose and outcomes.
    - ◆ *Explain* the info, protocol, and logistics.
    - ◆ *Transition* by saying, "Let's get started!"
- ◆ Repeat, making more eye contact with your reflection and reading less each time.
- ◆ Repeat three more times. Make progressively more eye contact with the mirror and less with your script.

Notice, by the third or fourth repetition, do you sound much smoother? Have you heard and overcome some unexpected verbal stumbles? Practicing out loud is much different, and more beneficial, than practicing in your head.

During the first three minutes of your class, your Kite will either effectively launch, or it will flounder. Once it's down, a Kite is harder to re-launch. What happens at this early stage is up to you … *and it's all about practice.*

CHAPTER 4
The Sail: Context

Summary

1. Crafting an Attention-getting Hook (pages 41–50)

Using a Hook immediately engages your participants and gets their brains ready to learn. It should be:
- Relatively short.
- Connected to the session's topic or purpose.
- Connected to who your participants are.
- Emotional, even if only mildly so.
- Inclusive.

2. Ensuring that Introductions Add Value (pages 51–54)

Ensure that your own introduction focuses on the results and benefits of what you do. Plan participant introductions so that they add value instead of leeching time or energy from your class.

3. Providing Essential Information about the Class (pages 55–56)

The more concise and necessary the information you give, the better. Be sure to include behavioral expectations to prevent turbulence later on in the class.

4. Creating a Strong Transition (page 57)

Always include a very short one-liner that connects the context to the body of your Kite. A smooth transition is the mark of a confident and professional trainer.

To download the worksheets you used in this chapter, go to www.guilamuir. com/kite-resources/ and enter your special password (**Kiteresources**).

In the next chapter, you will build your Kite's body. This will be both fun (because you get to choose great activities to bring your content alive) and easy (because it's all about what you know best—your topic.)

Chapter 5

The Sail
Body

Imagination is the highest kite one can fly.
Lauren Bacall

Overview

You're ready to design the most exciting part of your Kite's sail. The body is the most eye-catching, and largest, part of your Kite. It is the part:

- In which your knowledge and expertise shine.
- In which activities bring your content alive.
- That is the most fun for everyone, including you.

You can start building the body the minute you feel satisfied with your Kite's frame (its purpose and outcomes).

In fact, by building your learning outcomes, you already gained many insights about what content (and maybe even which activities) that this part of the sail should include.

However, if your Kite's frame is weak, its body will be weak too. If your purpose and outcomes are flabby or ill constructed, your Kite's body will sag and you will struggle to get it airborne. If you followed the steps in Chapter 1 and carefully constructed your frame, your Kite will be sturdy enough to support this large part of the sail.

What's in the Body?

Your Kite's sail is made up of broad stripes, stitched together seamlessly. Each stripe represents one learning outcome and contains these elements:

- Content
- Materials
- At least one activity per learning outcome

Your Kite's body, although it takes up the majority of your delivery time, is often the easiest part to develop. After all, you possess the content knowledge. All you need to do is download the content in your brain into each stripe on your Kite and choose an activity to help it come alive.

Let's examine each element. Then you'll have the opportunity to build your Kite's body.

1. Content

Definition: The content is the information you will convey about each learning outcome.

I used a real-life example in Chapter 1 of one trainer who developed her purpose statement and learning outcomes. I'd like to tell you the rest of that trainer's story. Here's what she'd developed so far:

Purpose
The purpose of this two-hour class is to help you communicate more effectively by writing clear and concise e-mails.

Outcomes
By the end of this session, you will be able to:

1. Explain the three most important e-mail etiquette rules.

2. Correct basic punctuation in several e-mails and be able to describe the rules used.

3. Compose and send an e-mail that integrates these etiquette and punctuation rules.

The trainer now needed to select appropriate content for each of the learning outcomes. Her first outcome alone (the one dealing with etiquette) could potentially include the content below, and more:

- Ensure the subject line is clear and descriptive
- Start with a greeting

- Use short paragraphs
- Do not overuse the Urgent option
- Proofread for grammar and spelling mistakes
- Avoid using slang and text language such as LOL
- Consider the message's tone
- Think twice before hitting "send"
- Sign off politely
- Use "reply," not "reply all."
- Do not copy or forward a message without permission.

The trainer had identified three outcomes for her two-hour class. She couldn't afford to load too much content into each outcome because of time constraints. Ultimately, she decided on these three "must-know" points for her first outcome ("By the end of this session, you will be able to explain the three most important e-mail rules").

- Use a clear and descriptive subject line
- Start with a greeting
- Think twice before hitting "send."

This trainer's first stripe on her Kite looked like this:

Example of a Stripe: Content

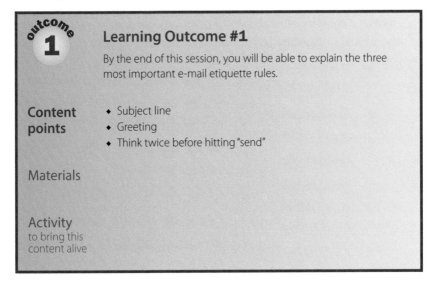

Outcome 1

Learning Outcome #1

By the end of this session, you will be able to explain the three most important e-mail etiquette rules.

Content points
- Subject line
- Greeting
- Think twice before hitting "send"

Materials

Activity
to bring this
content alive

What You Will Do

At this point, you need to figure out the correct type and amount of content to bring your learning outcome alive. This may be challenging. As one of my students put it, *"You gotta apply the acid test of 'must-know' versus 'nice-to-know.'"* "Must-know" content is the absolutely essential information that your participants need to achieve the outcome.

Consider how long your class will be. Then, as our trainer did in the example, list the absolute "must-know" pieces of content you *could* address in each learning outcome. It is highly likely that you will have to remove one or more content items to fit the time scheduled for your class.

Tip: Select only the "must-know" content points for each outcome. Leave out the "nice-to-know" extras. Leave your content in talking-point format for now; just use a few short words to capture it.

Congratulations! You have designed the first part of your stripe. You will use this same process to create all your stripes. And the more you do it, the easier it gets.

2. Materials

Definition: Materials are whatever you need to perform the activities you have selected. Materials can include slides, index cards, worksheets, handouts, or equipment necessary to practice new skills.

Take a look at what the trainer chose as her material for this learning outcome:

Example of a Stripe: Materials

outcome 1	**Learning Outcome #1** By the end of this session, you will be able to explain the three most important e-mail etiquette rules.
Content points	◆ Subject line ◆ Greeting ◆ Think twice before hitting "send"
Materials	Workbook with examples.
Activity to bring this content alive	

What You Will Do

Figure out what materials your participants will need to help them accomplish the content points. Will you need to create new worksheets, handouts, slides, or URLS to link to? Will you provide objects that participants can see and touch? What equipment will you need?

3. Activities

Definition: Activities are things the participants *do* to achieve each learning outcome.

When you have taken a class, how many times have you secretly (or not so secretly) rolled your eyes because the lecture seemed endless? Have you ever wanted to escape the classroom, or simultaneously read e-mails and text during a Webinar, simply because the trainer "yakked" too much? Don't be like those trainers! Include at least one activity per stripe in your Kite to break up your lecture and bring your content alive.

Activities are what the participants do when your mouth is closed. They can take many forms and are extremely important for many reasons. Activities:

- ◆ Are the primary ways for the trainer to assess if the participants are "getting it."
- ◆ Allow the participants to experiment with and get comfortable with new content.

- Bring the content alive.
- Are the main vehicle to achieve the learning outcomes.
- Are really where learning occurs.

Law of the Stripe: Each stripe of your Kite must include at least one activity. The activity should allow participants to practice one or all of the content points you address in that stripe.

See pages 68–73 for some examples of activities you could use to bring your class or Webinar alive.

What You Will Do

Choose your activities so that they:

- Are time effective.
- Bring each outcome alive.
- Present participants with the right level of difficulty or challenge.
- Allow for a balance of activity and reflection.

Let's return to our real-life trainer one last time. Take a look at the activity she chose to flesh out her content and bring this learning outcome alive.

Example of a Stripe: Activity

<table>
<tr><td>

outcome 1
</td><td>

Learning Outcome #1

By the end of this class, you will be able to explain the three most important e-mail etiquette rules.
</td></tr>
<tr><td>

Content points
</td><td>

♦ Subject line
♦ Greeting
♦ Think twice before hitting "send"
</td></tr>
<tr><td>Materials</td><td>Workbook with examples</td></tr>
<tr><td>

Activity
to bring this content alive
</td><td>

Provide 3 example e-mails. Participants individually choose most appropriate subject lines and greetings for each situation. Debrief together.
</td></tr>
</table>

Here is another example of a stripe from a different organization. Note that in this case, the trainer chose the activity to relate specifically to this outcome's second content point:

<table>
<tr><td>

outcome 1
</td><td>

State Department of Transportation
Learning Outcome #1

By the end of this class, you'll be able to describe five types of Variable Message Systems (VMS) technologies and how each is used
</td></tr>
<tr><td>

Content points
</td><td>

1. What is VMS?

2. Five Types of VMS technology used.
  ♦ Flip disk
  ♦ Hybrid
  ♦ Fiber optic
  ♦ Light emitting diode
  ♦ Walk-in
</td></tr>
<tr><td>Materials</td><td>

PPTs with photos only.
PPT with type and definition on each slide
</td></tr>
<tr><td>

Activity
to bring this content alive
</td><td>

Worksheet or Quiz:
Match terms and definitions. Discuss each thoroughly.
</td></tr>
</table>

Five Activities for Onsite Classes and Webinars

I have provided five activities to get you started, clearly marking how to do them both onsite and via Webinar. Wherever possible, these activities:

- ◆ Are based in learning research.
- ◆ Appeal to a variety of learning styles.

By no means do I suggest that these activities are the only ones you should consider. There are many excellent books on the market focused solely on great learning activities. I list a few of my favorite books in the "Great Resources for Course Design and Active Training" section at the end of the book.

Law of the Stripe: Each stripe of your Kite must include at least one activity. The activity should allow participants to practice one or all of the content points you address in that stripe.

TWO FOUNDATIONAL ACTIVITIES

The first two activities, Do It and Small-group Work, form the bedrock of effective adult education. They are so essential and foundational that you can sprinkle them liberally throughout the body of your Kite.

1. Do It

Definition

Participants try out the skill as they would in the "real world."

Why It Works

By trying out new skills, participants find it easier to transfer and use the skills once the training is over. *Do It is perhaps the most important activity in the Kite-flying world.*

Can you imagine taking a class in CPR (cardiopulmonary resuscitation) totally by slideshow? Imagine never touching a CPR dummy or practicing the skills. How well do you think you'd be able to perform CPR in an emergency situation?

 During your class, make it a priority to provide your participants the opportunity to get their hands on equipment, computer programs, and anything else they will need to perform the skill once they finish the class.

Can your participants get quick hands-on practice during the Webinar? Assign them a simple, relevant task and give them a short amount of time to accomplish it. Avoid dead space by providing verbal and visual input as participants work. Debrief quickly by using two-way audio or the Chat function.

Caution: It's easy to lose focus (or even some participants) using Do It via Webinar. Make your expectations clear at the beginning of class, and limit the time you provide.

2. Small-group Work

Definition
Participants work together in groups of three to five.

Why It Works
Adults learn through interacting with others. Small-group activities force participants out of passively listening and into active processing.

 Things to do in small groups:

◆ Solve problems
◆ Work through a scenario
◆ Practice the new skills
◆ Discuss implementation, consequences, action steps, etc.

Instruct participants to use the Chat box. Be sure to use open-ended questions to elicit their insights. You can select one participant's remark, read it aloud, and ask the rest of the group to use the Polling function if they agree with that comment.

THREE MORE ACTIVITIES

The following three activities are easy and effective. Select from them, or use others that you know and like, to fulfill the Law of the Stripe.

3. Think, Pair, and Share

Definition

Participants process a relevant point with a partner.

Why It Works

Think, Pair, and Share is incredibly easy and effective. It:

- Helps store information in long-term memory.
- Allows participants to reflect and work through content.
- Increases individual accountability.
- Encourages shy participants and non-native speakers to participate more comfortably because they think first, then share.

You can sprinkle Think, Pair, and Shares several times throughout any training session to increase participation while reinforcing content.

How to Use This Technique

Before or after providing content, tell the participants to form pairs with the person sitting next to them. Tell them to process some relevant point in the material. Your instructions should force them to work through the topic's application to their own lives or work. Provide a total amount of time for the exercise—perhaps two minutes.

Select from the following verbs when you give instructions.

Turn to your partner and:

- Fix
- Do
- Figure out
- Fill in
- Share
- Explain
- Discuss (etc.)

Examples:

Please turn to your neighbor and …

- Tell her the most important fact you have learned in the last ten minutes and why.
- Find the "Insert HTML object" in the Word menu.

* Make up quick questions about what you've just learned. See whether the person next to you can answer your question.

Debrief the activity by asking pairs to report to the whole group.

Keep in Mind
Before doing a Think, Pair, and Share, carefully construct your instructions. Write them on the flipchart or post on slides as you introduce the exercise.

 Instead of pairing, ask the participants to respond to your instructions as a group, using either two-way audio or the chat box.

4. Cards in Categories

Definition
Participants categorize cards under headings that are posted on the wall and then discuss the issues along with the choices they made.

Why It Works
This technique offers a great opportunity to reinforce new knowledge after you introduce a new content section. It also addresses visual, kinesthetic, and auditory ways of processing information.

How to Use This Technique
 On 8½" x 11" paper, prepare relevant headings for your content, one heading per paper.

Here are some examples:

TRUE, FALSE
LEGAL, ILLEGAL
[Name of] CATEGORY ONE, [Name of] CATEGORY TWO, [Name of] CATEGORY THREE, [Name of] CATEGORY FOUR, etc.

Post these on the wall before delivering your content. Ensure there is plenty of room on the wall for the participants to post many cards under each heading.

Based on your content, prepare cards by writing words, concepts, or phrases that would fall into one of the headings. Ensure that participants have a way of easily sticking their cards up under each heading (perhaps pre-tape the cards, or provide pieces of tape by sticking them on the wall, or use Post-Its as cards for a less re-usable exercise.)

Distribute cards, facedown, to all participants or teams. There is no limit to the number of cards each team or participant may receive.

Instruct participants to get out of their chairs and post their cards in the correct categories, based on the content you have provided.

When all the cards are posted, tell the participants to remain standing around the posted cards. Ask one participant to read each card out loud. Explore to see if each card was posted in the correct category. Facilitate a dialogue around the cards, moving them to the other category if directed by the participants. Bring out new insights, thoughts, and questions about the subject.

Keep in Mind

You can use Cards in Categories as a fun pre-test before delivering content. To use it as a post-test, ask the participants to change and correct the cards' locations after you deliver content.

 In the participants' workbook, provide the same type of headings. On screen, flash a concept, word, or element that must be categorized. Instruct participants to write that element under the correct heading in their workbooks. Discuss and correct responses using two-way audio.

Integrate activities every two to five minutes in an online environment.

5. Guided Note-taking

Definition

Instructor delivers a short lecture while participants fill in the missing words.

Why It Works

This technique is just a step up from passive listening, but it effectively engages the participants' brains. It's used best to capture the most important take-away ideas from a short lecture.

How to Use This Technique

Distribute handouts in which important words are left out. Tell the participants that you will now give a short lecture. Instruct them to write these words in the blanks as they hear them.

During your lecture, say exactly what's on the page. Before moving to the next point, lead a participatory dialogue with the class. Make it clear when you are moving to the next point.

When complete, briefly review the sentences in which the participants have written the missing words. Discuss this content to reinforce it.

Keep in Mind

The success of this activity, like all activities, depends on how you introduce it. Stress that by writing important points, participants remember them better. If you say something like, "You probably haven't done this since second grade," the activity will flop.

Speak slowly enough for the participants to keep up. Monitor them by watching as they write. Be sure to conduct a two-way conversation between points. Use this technique for only ten sentences or less, and make sure there is room enough for the participants to write each word on the handout.

In the participant workbook, provide a worksheet with missing words, as above. Give the lecture while showing slides with the missing word highlighted, one concept per slide. Encourage dialogue between slides.

Practice with Stripes

Use the worksheet below to scribble down preliminary ideas for content, activities, and materials for each of your learning outcomes.

Steps for using the worksheet:

- ◆ Be clear if you will be teaching onsite or via Webinar. You will choose different activities for each.
- ◆ Write each of your learning outcomes in the space provided.
- ◆ For each learning outcome, brainstorm content points. It's OK to have too many at this stage—you can remove excess points later.
- ◆ Choose one or two potential activities from pages 68–73 for each learning outcome. Or, use your own ideas for activities. Whatever you choose, the activities should reinforce each learning outcome.
- ◆ Jot down what materials will be necessary to carry out this activity.

Remember, this is your first draft. It should be messy. Choose activities that intuitively seem to fit best. You can always change them later. Have fun!

Worksheet: Practice with Your Stripes

Learning Outcome #1

By the end of this class, you will be able to:

Content points	Materials	Activity
		to bring this content alive

Worksheet: Practice with Your Stripes

Learning Outcome #2

By the end of this class, you will be able to:

Content points	Materials	Activity
		to bring this content alive

Learning Outcome #3

By the end of this class, you will be able to:

Content points	Materials	Activity
		to bring this content alive

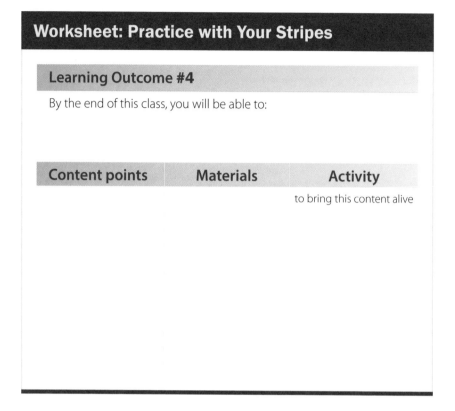

You have created the first draft of your Kite's body. How do you feel? Take some time to look this over before going to the final template in this chapter. Make sure that your chosen content points are the "must-know" chunks that participants need in order to achieve each learning outcome.

Template: More Details for Your Kite's Body

You have designed each stripe of your Kite's body. The following template provides more space for you to flesh out and include further detail in your content. What will you say for each talking point? What information will you convey?

Remember to stay within the boundaries of the talking points you have selected. You chose these specific "must-know" points for a reason. Fill in each enlarged stripe below. *Remember—include at least one activity per outcome.*

I have provided space for three learning outcomes. If you have more outcomes, just download more templates at www.guilamuir.com/kite-resources/.

Template: More Details for Your Kite's Body

1st Learning Outcome (from page 32)

By the end of this class, you will be able to:

_____

_____

Content:

_____

_____

_____

_____

_____

Activities:

_____

_____

_____

_____

_____

Materials Needed:

_____

_____

_____

_____

Approximate Time Needed to Achieve This Outcome:

_____

Template: More Details for Your Kite's Body

2nd Learning Outcome (from page 32)

By the end of this class, you will be able to:

_____

_____

Content:

_____

_____

_____

_____

Activities:

_____

_____

_____

_____

Materials Needed:

_____

_____

_____

_____

Approximate Time Needed to Achieve This Outcome:

_____

Template: More Details for Your Kite's Body

3rd Learning Outcome (from page 32)

By the end of this class, you will be able to:

_____

_____

Content:

_____

_____

_____

_____

_____

Activities:

_____

_____

_____

_____

Materials Needed:

_____

_____

_____

_____

Approximate Time Needed to Achieve This Outcome:

_____

Additional Resources for Online Trainers

🖥 Notes on Interactivity for Online Trainers

Interactivity … is not just asking a question; it's using the tools that come with your specific virtual-classroom platform as much as possible and in new and ingenious ways.

Murdoch/Muller, *The Learning Explosion*

Different Webinar platforms provide different functions. In the sections marked with the Webinar icon throughout this book, I have included *only* those online activities that you can use successfully with the simplest and most inexpensive Webinar platforms. If your organization has a more sophisticated online training system (one that offers more than simple Chat, Raise Hands, and Polling functions), just use these simple ideas to get your own creative juices flowing.

No matter how sophisticated your online training platform, you can ensure that your sessions are engaging and interactive by following these four guidelines:

1. ALWAYS PROVIDE INSTRUCTIONS BOTH VERBALLY AND VISUALLY.

Give instructions for every activity verbally as well as on a slide.

2. AVOID DEAD SPACE.

The online environment is like old-fashioned radio in one major way: You need to avoid dead space (silence) as much as possible. When you ask an open-ended question, e.g., "What are your experiences with …?" be patient. Typically, participants need from about thirty seconds to one minute to think, type, and send a response in the Chat box.

But instead of nervously awaiting input in total silence, you could provide examples on a slide *while* participants are typing their responses to your question. Although doing so breaks an important rule in an onsite classroom ("do one thing at a time"), multi-tasking can work well in a Webinar. You can also add helpful URLs to the Chat box as participants respond to a question.

3. PLAN YOUR ACTIVITIES WITH TIME RESTRAINTS IN MIND.

Depending on the number of participants, an activity that could take fifteen minutes in a classroom could take three times as long in an online environment. Plan and test your activities carefully to ensure that they will fit into your Webinar's time frame.

4. WARM UP AND COOL DOWN.

Open the Webinar five minutes before the class begins. (Some online trainers call this "meeting in the lobby.") Welcome and chat informally with the participants. Introduce them to the Webinar tools and to each other. This casual interaction goes a long way to increase participation and interaction during the Webinar. Be ready to re-introduce the tools once the Webinar officially begins.

After the class, throw a five-minute "after party" by inviting participants to stay online. Invite them to unmute, ask final questions, and talk informally with you and each other. The after-party is comparable to the time participants spend hanging around after an onsite class exchanging contact information and asking you any remaining questions.

Beyond these guidelines, ensure that your Webinar is active and participatory by:

- Intimately knowing your Webinar platform and what tools it provides.
- Asking open-ended question to elicit participant responses and insights throughout.
- Commenting on responses you see in the Chat box.
- Having participants chat among themselves and with you.
- Doing something interactive every two to five minutes.
- Always supplying a workbook, not just a compilation of slides but a manual that participants will actively write in.
- Using many different kinds of visuals: photographs, drawings, videos (if possible), and graphs; not just words.
- Always encouraging verbal responses from your participants and discouraging continual use of the muting function, if their environments allow this.
- Asking open-ended questions and never answering them yourself.
- Calling participants by name.

Worksheet for Online Trainers

 What are other ways to make Webinars as interactive as possible?

_____

_____

_____

_____

_____

_____

_____

_____

_____

_____

_____

_____

_____

_____

_____

_____

_____

_____

_____

_____

CHAPTER 5
The Sail: Body

Summary

1. The body of your Kite is where you deliver content and information about your subject.

2. To design the body, think of each outcome as being a stripe on the Kite, stitched seamlessly to the other stripes. Each stripe contains:
   - Content
   - Materials
   - At least one activity to bring that outcome alive.

3. Know that it will take more time to do participatory activities during a Webinar than onsite. At the same time, Webinar participants expect the training to move swiftly. Plan your activities accordingly. Avoid dead air space.

4. Whether onsite or for a Webinar, be sure to time-test your activities before your first class.

To download the templates and worksheets you used in this chapter, go to www.guilamuir.com/kite-resources/ and enter your special password (**Kiteresources**).

Congratulations! You have just completed building your Kite's sail, its most visible and dynamic part. You're ready to move to the final building phase, your Kite's tail. Your Kite is almost ready for its test flight!

Chapter 6

The Tail
Active Closure

Don't ignore the small things. The kite flies because of its tail.
Hawaiian proverb

Active Closure

Think of the kites you see on a windy day. Their gorgeous and unique tails serve an essential purpose. Without tails, kites are unstable and will crash.

The only way to avoid your Kite's crashing is to construct and attach a tail. It completes your Kite's dynamic appearance while ensuring that your Kite stays aloft.

The tail you'll develop in this section is called "active closure." An active closure provides a final opportunity to:

- reinforce your participants' knowledge and skills
- test understanding
- solidify retention, and
- leave a great impression.

An active closure keeps your class energized and aloft to the very end.

Transition to Active Closure

Just as you transitioned from the context part of your Kite's sail to its body by saying *"So, let's get started!"* you need to make a smooth transition from your Kite's body to its tail. Doing so is easy. Just pick one of the following sentences and make it your own:

"In conclusion, …"

"To close, let's …"

"So, let's tie everything up by …"

> ### What will I say to transition from my Kite's body to its tail?
>
> Write it here:
>
> _____
>
> _____
>
> _____
>
> _____
>
> _____

Choosing a Tail That Works

To create your active closure, you can choose from two broad categories of activities:

- Outcome-based Assessments
- Review and Bridge

For an even more robust closure, you can combine options from both these categories.

An active closure can take up to 10 percent of total class time. Be sure *always* to design enough time for closure.

Active Closure: Outcome-based Assessments

Using your learning outcomes is a great way to assess how well your participants can do what you promised they'd be able to do by the end of class. Using the outcomes ensures accountability. If you notice that participants still can't perform the learning outcomes as well as you would like, you still have the opportunity to review and reinforce the new information before class ends.

1. "Ask the Outcomes"

Turn the learning outcomes into directives. Use the directives to test the participants.

Here are some examples:

- "Please name the five most important steps to take as you wait for the ambulance to respond."

- "In order, demonstrate the three steps in troubleshooting a HAR System."

- "Describe how to prevent power-line contact and what to do if contact occurs."

 Verbally ask small groups or individuals to do what the verb in the outcome indicates.

 Provide a quiz using these questions either during the Webinar or immediately afterward, using an online survey tool such as Survey Monkey.

2. Outcome-based Evaluation.

This type of evaluation reflects participants' evaluation of their own learning.

 Prepare an evaluation form based on the learning outcomes for the class. Ask your participants to evaluate their own learning on each learning outcome, using a scale of 1–5. Also, request their comments about each learning outcome. (See the two examples on pages 91 and 92. Note that in Example #1 the participants also evaluate how well the class met its stated purpose, which is important feedback for you.)

You can:

- Make the outcome-based evaluation more of a recall test by asking specific questions about each outcome (see Example #2 on page 92).

- Use an outcome-based evaluation both at the beginning and at the end of class to measure perceived progress in learning. The evaluation then becomes a pre- and post-assessment.

- Note the outcomes on which many participants rate themselves the lowest. This is a great indication that this part of your class is not yet robust enough. The problem could be either a design issue (the learning outcome is not specific) or a delivery issue (you are not teaching this stripe clearly). Try tweaking both your learning outcome and the way you deliver it.

 Follow the same guidelines to design and use a survey using an online tool, like Survey Monkey.

Review and Bridge: Two Options

In this type of active closure, participants either create action plans to use new skills in the real world or review past material and ask questions before moving to the next part of the class.

1. My Commitments

- Ask participants what they will do *more of, less of, or differently* as a result of the class. (See Example #3 on page 93.)

- Explain that you'd like them to write at least two commitments for themselves.

- When everyone is finished, ask participants to verbally share their commitments (depending on class size) to the class as a whole, with their tablemates, or with a partner. They should preface each commitment by voicing a strong "I *will* _____."

 Give participants enough time to record their responses in their workbooks. Then, using two-way audio, ask each to make his or her verbal commitments to the group as a whole. Alternatively, they can simply record their commitments in the chat box.

2. Two Insights, One Area of Confusion
(for ongoing or sequential classes)

This short exercise is a helpful way to evaluate student learning and use that information to customize the following session.

 Distribute index cards to everyone. Instruct participants to write two insights they received from this session, as well as one area in which they're still confused. Collect and read the comments and tweak your next session accordingly.

 Instruct participants to send you their responses using the chat function. Print the responses and distribute them to the participants before the next class session.

In designing your active closure, remember not to "crash your Kite." Always design plenty of time to summarize, reinforce, and clarify before ending your class.

Worksheet: My Active Closure

Which of the options on pages 91–93 will I use to end my class? What other ideas do I have to reinforce the information in an active way?

_____

_____

_____

_____

_____

_____

_____

_____

_____

_____

_____

_____

_____

_____

_____

_____

_____

_____

_____

_____

Additional Resources on Active Closure

EXAMPLE #1: Outcome-based Evaluation
Meetings That Work: The Art of Facilitation

The purpose of this training was to provide essential skills to ensure that your meetings are productive.

How well did this workshop achieve its overall purpose? Please rate it from 1 (not at all) to 5 (completely).

1	2	3	4	5
Not at all				Completely

Now please rate how well **you** can do the following as a result of this workshop:

I can describe the "facilitator frame of mind" and explain when the roles of content expert and facilitator are appropriate.

1	2	3	4	5
Not at all				Well

I can describe the benefits of using an outcome-based agenda and develop one to keep my next meeting on track.

1	2	3	4	5
Not at all				Well

I can demonstrate at least seven essential facilitator skills.

1	2	3	4	5
Not at all				Well

I can describe a minimum of five ways to respond effectively to difficult group dynamics.

1	2	3	4	5
Not at all				Well

What was particularly helpful about the training?

_____

_____

What was not helpful?

_____

_____

EXAMPLE #2: Outcome-based Evaluation
INTEGRATED PEST MANAGEMENT (IPM):
Best Management Practices Post-class Survey

Please rate yourself on how well you can do the following things, where 1 indicates "I cannot do this at all," and 5 indicates "I am confident in my ability to do this".

As a result of this course, **I CAN:**

1. Name the 3 main types of pests we deal with in Seattle parks.

1   2   3   4   5

What are these pests?

1. _____

2. _____

3. _____

2. List the 5 components in an Integrated Pest Management (IPM) program.

1   2   3   4   5

List them here:

1. _____

2. _____

3. _____

4. _____

5. _____

3. Describe an IPM program for the pest we discussed in class.

1   2   3   4   5

Include all phases of the program:

_____

_____

_____

_____

EXAMPLE #3: Action Plan
Using My New Facilitation Skills

In the planning and facilitation of my next meeting, I will do these three things *differently* than I have in the past:

1._____

_____

_____

_____

_____

2._____

_____

_____

_____

_____

3._____

_____

_____

_____

_____

CHAPTER 6
The Tail: Active Closure

Summary

An active closure provides a final opportunity to:

- reinforce your participants' knowledge and skills
- test understanding
- solidify retention, and
- leave a great impression.

An active closure keeps your class energized and aloft to the very end.

To create your active closure, you can choose from two broad categories of activities: Each category offers two choices. Choose the closure that works best for each class you develop.

1. Outcome-based Assessments

- Ask the Outcomes
- Use an Outcome-based Evaluation.

2. Review and Bridge

- My Commitments
- Two Insights, One Area of Confusion (for ongoing or sequential classes.)

To download the worksheets and resources you used in this chapter, go to www.guilamuir.com/kite-resources/ and enter your special password (**Kiteresources**).

Chapter 7

Putting It All Together

Finalizing your Kite design

You will now integrate all the information you have put into templates into one document. This is your Kite template. It serves as your class's detailed outline. It also serves as the script for your class's trial launch.

Although you can still revise this document up to the very minute you launch your class, this final document should include everything you have created so far. Be as detailed as you like. Remember, you can also download the template at www.guilamuir.com/kite-resources/.

CONTEXT

Hook
Intro

Info
Transition

LEARNING OUTCOMES

outcome
1

outcome
2

outcome
3

content
materials
activities

content
materials
activities

content
materials
activities

BODY

CLASS PURPOSE

CLOSURE

Kite Class Template: Context

Class Title:

_____

Length of Class:

_____

My HOOK

_____

_____

_____

_____

_____

_____

_____

My INTRO

_____

_____

_____

_____

PURPOSE
The purpose of this training is to …

_____

_____

_____

Kite Class Template: Context

LEARNING OUTCOMES
By the end of the session, you will be able to …

_____

_____

_____

_____

_____

Participant INTROS
What will you do?

_____

_____

_____

Info, Expectations, and Logistics

_____

_____

_____

_____

Transition to Content

_____

_____

Continue to **Kite Class Template: Body**

Kite Class Template: Body

1st Learning Outcome
By the end of this section, you will be able to:

_____

_____

Content Talking Points:

_____

_____

_____

_____

_____

_____

_____

Activities:

_____

_____

_____

_____

_____

_____

_____

Approximate Time Needed to Achieve This Outcome:

_____

Kite Class Template: Body

2nd Learning Outcome
By the end of this section, you will be able to:

_____

_____

Content Talking Points:

_____

_____

_____

_____

_____

_____

_____

Activities:

_____

_____

_____

_____

_____

_____

Approximate Time Needed to Achieve This Outcome:

_____

Kite Class Template: Body

3rd Learning Outcome
By the end of this section, you will be able to:

_____

_____

Content Talking Points:

_____

_____

_____

_____

_____

_____

_____

Activities:

_____

_____

_____

_____

_____

Approximate Time Needed to Achieve This Outcome:

_____

Transition to Closure:

_____

_____

Kite Class Template: Closure

Active Closure
(What will you do?)

_____

_____

_____

_____

_____

_____

To download the Kite Class Template, go to www.guilamuir.com/kite-resources/ and enter your special password (**Kiteresources**).

Congratulations!
You Have Finished Designing Your Kite

Look over your template. Now that you captured all your ideas, do all the pieces fit together? Do the stripes seamlessly flow from one to the next? Does the active closure review and reinforce the entire Kite?

You may well have to do at least one trial run before your first training session. You can do this with a small group of people who share some characteristics with your intended participants. Also, consider inviting a few experts in this topic to join your pilot audience. Use this group's feedback to tweak or shorten your activities and make final revisions.

Once you do a trial run, you are ready to set sail.

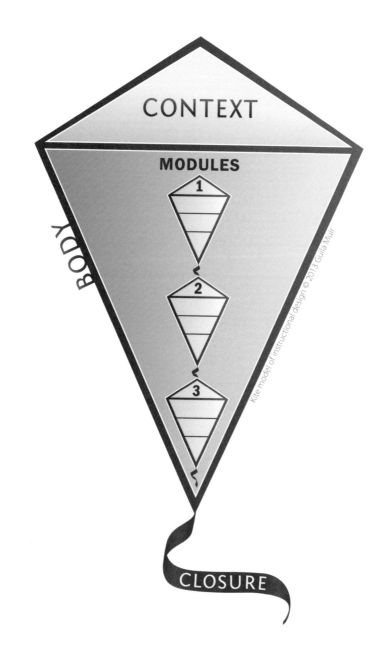

Kite model of instructional design © 2013 Gulia Muir

Chapter 8

Developing Longer Training Sessions

Using the Kite Method to design much longer courses

Kite design ranges from small and simple to large and complex.
Troy Griepentrog, Mother Earth News

The Kite template is extraordinarily flexible. Although most people use it to design classes, seminars, and workshops lasting from one hour up to one day, others have used the template to design much longer training sessions.

Using the Kite template, you can design training sessions of any length. Simply use a slightly modified version of the process outlined so far.

How to Do It

Let's say you have determined the problem, know the participants, and need to design a six-week training session. Consider that six-week session your "Big Kite."

1. First, create your Big Kite's

   ◆ Purpose (pages 22–24)
   ◆ Outcomes (pages 25–31)
   ◆ Context (pages 40–58)

2. Then: Turn each of the outcomes you have created for your Big Kite into a purpose statement for one of its "mini-Kites," or modules. Doing this may sound confusing at first, but is actually quite easy to do. Here's an example.

Big Kite outcome #1: *By the end of this six-week session, you will be able to perform all necessary adjustments to the equipment.*

Transformed into one "mini-Kite's" purpose statement: *The purpose of this one-week-long module is to teach you to perform all necessary adjustments to the equipment.*

3. Once you have created the purpose statement for each "mini-Kite," develop its learning outcomes (pages 25–31). You will develop a stripe for each learning outcome. Remember, each stripe contains:

   ◆ Content (page 62)
   ◆ Materials (page 64)
   ◆ Activities (page 65)

Finish each module with a quick active closure (pages 87–89).

Note: You will improve each "mini-Kite" (module) if you can supply it with a Hook. **However, don't sweat this!** It's much more important that its frame (purpose and learning outcomes) are strong and robust and that each module helps to achieve your Big Kite's purpose.

4. Once you have developed each stripe, create your Big Kite's active closure (page 87—89).

Using the Kite Method to design longer sessions keeps your training outcome-focused and active. You'll keep yourself, and your participants, energized for the long run.

PART FOUR

FLYING YOUR KITE

Out of the hand and into flight,
Its colors brilliant and bright ...

Lynn Davis

Chapter 9

Launching Your Kite

The exciting day has come. You are now ready to launch your Kite! What skills will you need to keep it aloft?

Whether onsite or online, these three strategies are key:

- Have a flight plan.
- Prepare for turbulence.
- Fly your kite with your whole body.

1. Have a Flight Plan

The surest way to crash your Kite is to make assumptions about the environment in which you will fly it.

Assumptions That Will Crash Your Kite

 Onsite   **Online**

Onsite	Online
If you send a room diagram, the space will be set up correctly by the time you arrive.	If you "sort of" understand how to run a Webinar, all will go without a hitch.
All the technology will be compatible.	Your network connection is always dependable.
The space doesn't matter; the content's what's important.	Your participants have all the equipment they need and know how to use it.
You'll do this training the same way, no matter who shows up.	You'll do this training the same way, no matter who shows up.

Use this Flight Plan Checklist before each launch. It will help ensure your Kite stays out of the trees.

Flight Plan Checklist

❑ View the room *before* your training day.

❑ Know who your participants are. When possible, send out a survey to discover their specific characteristics, needs, anxieties, previous experiences, level of expertise, etc.

❑ Oversee the room setup.

❑ Ensure that all the technology works.

❑ Find out how to control the temperature.

❑ Arrive at least forty-five minutes early on the training day.

❑ Rehearse in the room; practice the first five minutes of your class *out loud.*

❑ Deeply know your Webinar platform. Practice all the tools and be ready to use them.

❑ Know who your participants are. When possible, send out a survey to discover their specific characteristics, needs, anxieties, previous experiences, level of expertise, etc.

❑ Double-check your network connection and have a backup plan.

❑ Test all the technical components of your platform at least one hour before training begins.

❑ Close out sources of noise or interruption.

❑ Practice the first five minutes of your class out loud.

2. Prepare for Turbulence

I fully appreciate the ability of trees to attract kites. They have special powers that way.

> Charlie Denton
> NASA Engineer and Master Kite Builder

Turbulence is rough air you encounter once your Kite is aloft. It could take the form of a participant's non-responsive or resistant behavior, technology or logistical glitches, a dominating speaker, or (rarely) open hostility. Prepare yourself intellectually, emotionally, and physically to deal with turbulence before it occurs. Make sure you:

- Know your stuff. Be prepared for as many questions and challenges as possible.

- Have used your Flight Plan Checklist to prepare the environment.

- Have rehearsed the context section of your Kite, *out loud,* at least three times (see pages 58—59).

- Try to transform any nervousness you may feel into excitement.

- Be ready with a few alternative activities that you could substitute for the ones you have planned, "just in case."

- Have had enough to eat and drink.

- Don't take turbulence personally. Where possible, fix the problem and move on.

To Prevent Turbulence

Your behavior is key to preventing turbulence before it occurs. By establishing clear expectations and modeling both dominance and cooperation as a trainer, you set your Kite up for clear sailing.

Clear Expectations

As discussed in Part Three, being clear about your behavioral expectations for participants will calm the wind before you launch. Your expectations for both onsite and online environments are probably similar. Expectations could reference:

- Use of cell phones and electronic devices during class

- How you will deal with questions and comments

- Participant involvement during the session
- Timing of breaks
- Mute or unmute audio

State clearly what you expect from the participants, and ask for their questions regarding those expectations before going on.

Your Own Behavior: What Are You Expressing?

Another way to prevent and control turbulence during your class is to model two seemingly polarized behaviors: dominance and cooperation.

1. Dominance

Dominance doesn't mean forceful or heavy-handed control. Instead, it refers to your ability to provide your participants with strong guidance and clear consequences. This guidance includes:

- Stating the learning outcomes clearly.
- Providing clear instructions, both visually and verbally.
- Making expectations about behavior clear.
- Following through with consequences. (Online example: If someone has muted his phone connection, call him by name and request that he un-mute.)

Onsite, it's important to use assertive body language. Maintain an erect posture. Speak deliberately and clearly, especially in the face of inappropriate behavior. Keep your cool.

Online, re-state and show your expectations for participation on a slide.

Make sure you are training with as few background interruptions as possible.

2. Cooperation

Cooperation refers to your ability to show you care about your participants' needs and opinions. It highlights a sense of teamwork. Cooperation involves:

- Taking a personal and authentic interest in participants.
- Learning about participants' interests and passions outside of class.

- Talking informally before and after class.
- Greeting each participant by name.
- Asking questions and responding to the answers you get.

When you model both dominance and cooperation as a trainer, you greatly reduce the potential for turbulence.

3. Fly Your Kite with Your Whole Body

Imagine yourself flying a kite outdoors on a windy day. Feel the strength of your core muscles as you strain against the wind. Feel the happy pull of your arm muscles as you guide the string. When you fly a kite, you are physically committed and focused.

That's how you need to be when you present your training, too. Whether onsite or online, the act of presenting is highly physical. It involves not just your head, but your heart and body as well.

> Guideline: Many professional speakers practice their entire presentation *five to seven times, out loud and on their feet,* before considering themselves ready to deliver it to an audience.

 ## Physical Skills for Onsite Training

When people describe the best trainer they've ever seen, the word "energy" always comes up. Here are two secrets of exuding energy, vitality, the life force, as a trainer.

1. Be Big

Regardless of what size you are, *take up more room.* Become the "Intensified You." Practice in front of a mirror:

- Stand up straight.
- Use your arms and hands to create space around your body.
- Pump up the volume in your voice. Try saying, "Hello! My name is …," in a healthy and robust voice.
- Pour yourself in. Be 100 percent present.

Practice "being big" before you get in front of a group.

2. Come Alive in the Magic Circle

Once you stand up and speak, you step into the "magic circle." This is your space to shine. This little patch of earth is your own personal piece of real estate—so own it. Show what you've rehearsed. Be big, take up room, and pour the energy on.

When you step out of the magic circle, you can relax. You no longer have to take up space ... you can go home and "be little" as you watch TV, putter in the garden, or hang out with the kids. But you owe it to your participants to shine when you're in the magic circle.

Physical Skills for Online Training

You may think that because your participants can't see you, you can afford to be a slouch. The opposite is true! Your participants will take their behavioral cues from you. Because participants can't see your physical cues, you must use your voice to express your commitment to, and excitement about, your subject.

> Caution to online trainers: Remember that your Webinar is a training session, not a sales pitch. Shun marketing phrases (example: "Buy it now!") and overheated excitement (e.g., talking fast and rarely taking a breath). Be vibrant while keeping a conversational tone. Take care not to shout into the microphone.

Practice your voice before class begins: How clear, committed, and enthusiastic can it be? Consider standing. Presentation skills experts have said that we are **at least 50 percent less dynamic** when sitting down because our body movements are halved. Your entire body is more restricted, and it's even more difficult to breathe properly. This makes it harder to project your voice.

In a poll conducted by George Piskurich,[1] learners stated that the best online teachers used humor, exhibited a high degree of interpersonal skills, provided feedback, and managed online discussions well.

Remember—it's all about grace, strength, and power as a trainer. Use your physical self to keep that Kite in the air.

Exercise: Try Flying Your Kite with Your Whole Body

Note: If you haven't already filled out your Kite template on pages 96–101, you are not yet ready to take this next step.

It's time to test-fly your Kite in the safety of your office or home. Go back to your Kite template, in which you put together all the elements of your class (pages 96–101). Print it out if you can. Your template now becomes your script as you launch your Kite for the first time.

Get Ready!

- Stand up.
- Get a timer, whether it is an app on your phone, a stopwatch, or an egg timer from the kitchen. Set it for five minutes. Do not start it yet.
- Go to a full-length mirror (if possible) and stand in front of it.
- Plant your feet straight ahead. Look yourself in the eye. Smile.
- Draw your shoulders down your back, opening your chest.
- Let your eyes travel downward. Check out your body. Are you slouching, putting all your weight on one hip, or closing your hands in front of your stomach or abdomen? Stand up straight. Open your arms slightly away from your body.

Get Set!

- Hold your Kite template in your left hand. Do not allow your hands to come together in front of your body at any time during these five minutes.

Go!

- Start the timer.
- State your class's **title** and its **length** out loud. Your voice should be robust and strong. (As you do this, your voice may sound overly loud and potentially strange. That's OK! You will need to be louder than you think once you are in front of your participants. You might as well practice increasing your volume now.)
  - Then, following the flow of content in your Kite template,
    - **Hook** your learners as if they are right in front of you. Make eye contact with your reflection.

Exercise: Try Flying Your Kite with Your Whole Body

- *Introduce* yourself using your benefits-based introduction.
- *State* the session's purpose.
- *Explain* the info, protocol, and logistics.
- *State* the session's learning outcomes. Remember to speak as if you were addressing your participants. Make eye contact with yourself.
- *Simulate* how you would instruct the participants to introduce themselves.
- *Explain* any further information about the training, expectations, and logistics.
- *Transition* into your content by saying, "So let's get started!"

Start Your Content Section

- *State* the first learning outcome again.
- *Start* talking about your subject. Use your talking points as a guide.
- *Introduce* your activity. Provide clear instructions to accomplish it. If you have remaining time, then:
- *State* the second learning outcome.
- *Start* talking about your subject. Use your talking points as a guide.
- *Introduce* your activity. Provide clear instructions to accomplish it.

Remember

- Transition into your conclusion by saying, "In conclusion," or "To close, …"
- Close your class.

When the timer goes off, stop. Sit down and rest. Review how this first practice went. Where did you stumble? What went great? Stand up and repeat up to five more times—just as the pros do!

To download copies of this exercise, go to www.guilamuir.com/kite-resources/ and enter your special password (**Kiteresources**).

Chapter 10

Post-flight Debrief

I make many changes, and reject and try again,
until I am satisfied.
Ludwig van Beethoven

Congratulations! You have successfully built, launched, and flown your Kite. How did it go? Will you do it again?

It's important to evaluate the flight once you've landed the Kite. You can do so immediately after the training, as well as weeks or months afterward.

How Will You Know if It Worked?

Did your Kite affect the problem you set out to address? Some trainers have the luxury of being able to directly observe their participants before and after the class. Are the participants doing things differently? You can also evaluate the training in other ways. Here are a few:

- ◆ Send a paper or online survey a few weeks after the training is finished, and again later on.
- ◆ Collect data before and after the training. Compare it. What, if anything, has changed? For example, are there fewer complaint calls or requests for technical support after the training?
- ◆ Are there requests for a repeat of the training session?

What are specific ways you could find out how effective your class was, taking your unique situation into account?

Also ask yourself about challenges that came up for you during the training. Did you experience technical problems? Did your Hook effectively engage? Was the room adequate? Did you discover that your own content knowledge was weak in one particular area? Did the activities flow smoothly?

It's important to stop and reflect before flying the Kite again. You can make improvements based on your findings. Then, you can start the process again:

- Is there still a need for training?

- Is the training purpose the same, or has the initial problem changed?

- Who should the participants be?

- Are the learning outcomes the same, or have needs changed since you delivered the training?

Real-life Evaluation

In Part Two of this book, I introduced you to three people who decided to build Kites in their areas of expertise. Here, we show how they evaluated the impact of their classes.

Who: Activity director, assisted living complex

Problem: Residents don't know how to use e-mail to connect with family members.

What will have changed: Those residents who wish to send e-mails can do so relatively easily.

Evaluation: The Activity director tracked the number of residents reporting if they felt comfortable sending e-mails after participating in a series of four, thirty-minute-long classes. Based on these reports, she offered volunteer-led, individualized tutoring on an ongoing basis as a follow-up to the training.

Who: Manager of Human Resources State Department of Revenue

Problem: An increased number of small business owners are calling because they're confused about how to file taxes under the new regulations.

What will have changed: We receive 50 percent fewer calls about this issue.

Evaluation: The Human Resource Department monitored the number of complaint calls received before and after the half-day class. To their delight, the number of complaint calls decreased by 47 percent.

Who: Software engineers, global corporation selling high-end measurement equipment

Problem: Several new clients have returned equipment because they can't use it properly.

What will have changed: All clients can confidently perform the most necessary measurement actions immediately upon setting up the equipment in their factories.

Evaluation: The engineers sent a brief survey to everyone they'd trained. In it, they asked participants to self-assess their skills before training and after the training. From these surveys, they realized that they needed to improve specific modules of their training to make them more user-friendly.

You're Ready to Re-launch!

You now own the tools and process you need to develop and deliver high-quality training—just by building and flying your Kite. Have fun as you fly it again and again.

Notes

PART ONE

1. One simplified approach to instructional design is the ADDIE Model. The acronym derives from five phases—Analysis, Design, Development, Implementation, and Evaluation. Here is one example of ADDIE:

ADDIE Model

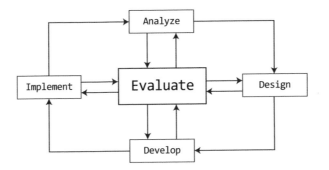

2. Concepts that otherwise would not be memorable can be placed easily into the brain through the use of metaphors. B. DePorter, M. Reardon, and S. Singer-Nourie, *Quantum Teaching: Orchestrating student success* (Boston: Allyn & Bacon, 1999).

From the perspective of the brain, a metaphor is a bridge between two ideas that, at least on the surface, are not related. Jonah Lehere, *Imagine* (New York: Houghton Mifflin Harcourt, 2012), 10.

PART TWO

1. Robert Mager, *Making Instruction Work*, 12.

PART FOUR, Chapter One

1. George M. Piskurich, *Rapid Instructional Design: Learning ID Fast and Right*, 383.

Resources

Downloadable Templates, Worksheets, Checklists, and Additional Resources

To download copies of all these resources, go to www.guilamuir.com/kite-resources/ and enter your special password (**Kiteresources**).

PART THREE: Building Your Kite

Great Resources for Course Design and Active Training

Internet Sites

Guila Muir's Train the Trainer blog:
www.guilamuir.com/train-the-trainer-articles

The Thiagi Group: *www.thiagi.com*

Sharon Bowman's website: *www.bowperson.com*

Vanderbilt Center for Teaching: *www.vanderbilt.edu/cft/resources/teaching_ resources/preparing/course_design.htm*

International Society for Performance Improvement (ISPI): *www.ispi.org*

Center for Accelerated Learning: *www.alcenter.com/alindex.html*

Eureka! Blog and Training Tips: *www.eureka-tp.com*

The Accidental Trainer: *www.theaccidentaltrainer.org*

Books

Ambrose, S., et al. *How Learning Works*. San Francisco: Jossey-Bass, 2010.

Angelo, T., and K. P. Cross. *Classroom Assessment Techniques: A handbook for college teachers*. San Francisco: Jossey-Bass, 1993.

Beyerlein, S., C. Holmes, and D. Apple. *Faculty Guidebook: A comprehensive tool for improving faculty performance*. Lisle, IL: Pacific Crest, 2006.

Bowman, S. *Preventing Death by Lecture!—Terrific tips for turning listeners into learners*. San Francisco: Jossey-Bass, 2001.

———. *The Ten-minute Trainer: 150 ways to teach it quick and make it stick!* San Francisco: Jossey-Bass, 2005.

Calderon, D., and K. Bellemare. *Wizbangers*. Victoria, BC: Trafford, 2005.

Dirksen, J. *Design for How People Learn*. Berkeley, CA: New Riders, 2012.

Fenwick, T., and J. Parsons. *The Art of Evaluation*. Buffalo, NY: Thompson Educational Publishing, 2000.

Fink, D. *Creating Significant Learning Experiences*. San Francisco: Jossey-Bass, 2003.

Gustafson, K., and R. Branch. *Survey of Instructional Development Models* 3rd edition. Syracuse, NY: ERIC Clearinghouse of Information and Technology, 1997.

Lucas, R. *The Creative Training Idea Book: Inspired tips and techniques for engaging and effective learning.* New York: Amacom, 2003.

Mager, R. *Making Instruction Work.* Atlanta, GA: CEP Press, 1997.

Meier, D. *The Accelerated Learning Handbook.* San Francisco: Pfeiffer, 2006.

Miner, N. *The Accidental Trainer: A reference manual for the small, part-time, or one-person training department.* San Francisco: Pfeiffer, 2006.

Murdoch, M., and T. Muller. *The Learning Explosion.* Salt Lake City, UT: Franklin Covey Co., 2011.

Piskurich, G. *Rapid Instructional Design: Learning ID fast and right.* San Francisco: Pfeiffer, 2006.

Pluth, B. *Webinars with Wow Factor: Tips, tricks and interactive activities for virtual training.* No city or publisher noted: 2010.

Rogoff, R. *The Training Wheel: A simple model for instructional design.* New York: John Wiley and Sons, 1987.

Rothwell, W., and H. Kazanas. *Mastering the Instructional Design Process: A systematic approach.* San Francisco: Jossey-Bass, 2008.

Silberman, M. *101 Ways to Make Training Active.* San Francisco: Pfeiffer, 2005.

Sivasailam, T. *Design Your Own Games and Activities: Thiagi's templates for performance improvement.* San Francisco: Pfeiffer, 2003.

———. *Thiagi's 100 Favorite Games.* San Francisco: Pfeiffer, 2005.

———. *Thiagi's Interactive Lectures.* Alexandria, VA: ASTD, 2006.

Stolovitch, H., and E. Keeps. *Telling Ain't Training.* Alexandria, VA: ASTD, 2002.

Sugar, S. *Games That Teach: Experiential activities for reinforcing training.* San Francisco: Pfeiffer, 1998.

Tate, M. *"Sit & Get" Won't Grow Dendrites: 20 professional learning strategies that engage the adult brain.* Thousand Oaks: 2004

Vai, M., and K. Sosulki. *Essentials of Online Course Design: A standards-based guide.* New York: Routledge, 2011.

Vella, J. *Training Through Dialogue: Promoting effective learning and change with adults.* San Francisco: Jossey-Bass, 1995.

Vella, J., P. Berardinelli, and J. Burrow. *How Do You Know They Know?* San Francisco: Jossey-Bass, 1998.

West, E. *The Big Book of Icebreakers.* New York: McGraw Hill, 1999.

Wick, C., R. Pollock, and R. Flanagan. *The Six Disciplines of Breakthrough Learning: How to turn training and development into business results.* San Francisco: Pfeiffer, 2006.

Appreciation

Enormous thanks to …

My parents, Pat Moore-Howard and Bob Howard, for the passion for teaching they passed on to me.

Carol Weaver for acting as my mentor.

Anne-Marie DeGeorge for her thoughtful editing and Sara Schneider for her intuitive, expert graphic design skills.

My partner, Rebecca DeGeorge, for suggesting that I write a book in 1985. Thanks for haranguing me about it only occasionally since then.

Julie Miller, Peggy Dolane, Darlene Pearsal, Lynda McDaniel, Virginia McCullough, Mary Ross, Catherine DeGeorge, Sharon Bowman, Julie Scandora, and Stephanie Martindale for their helpful insights.

My open-water swim companions, especially Laura Lee and Randy Perkins. Those shared, cold, exhilarating swims always help me "re-set" my brain.

And a special thanks to all my students for taking on the challenge of instructional design.

About the Author

Guila Muir is passionate about designing and delivering great adult education and enabling others to do so. As principal of Muir and Associates, she has enjoyed turning subject matter experts into great trainers for two decades. She began her career training Thai teachers in a refugee camp in 1981, and her clients include hundreds of global companies, municipalities, states, and non-profits.

Guila is also passionate about open-water swimming. Having learned to swim at age forty-six, she has swum from Alcatraz to San Francisco ten times. She sees strong parallels between the creativity, technicality, and pure physicality of swimming and the art of training.

Index